First published in 2024 by
Chadworth & Sons.

Copyright © Chadworth & Sons. Ltd. 2024

Design copyright © C. M. D. Whitwood

All rights reserved. This publication may not be reproduced, stored in a retrieval system or transmitted, in any form or by any means, electronic, mechanical, photocopying or otherwise, without the prior permission of the publishers.

ISBN: 9798301518737

Other titles available. Please visit:
www.chadworthandsons.com

Dedicated to all those who built, served and worshipped in these churches.

LIVING STONES

A history of the church,
parish and people of
St Joseph the Worker,
Sherburn-in-Elmet

Chris Whitwood

Contents

Timeline of Parish Priests	i
Foreword by Father Paul F. Moxon	iii
Introduction	v

Living Stones

The Promised Land	3
Foundations	27
Perserverance	45
Construction	65
Renewed and Built Up	85
The Poet Priest	101
Not an End, but a Beginning	123
In Reflection	141
Prayer to St Joseph for Workers	147
Acknowledgements	149

Timeline of Parish Priests

The Parish of The Immaculate Conception, Scarthingwell

1854 - 1861	Charles Augustus O'Neill
1861 - 1862	Henry Walker
1862 - 1864	John Dwyer
1864 - 1866	Henry J. Green
1866 - 1874	James Guthrie
1874 - 1877	John Scott
1877 - 1884	Thomas Worthy
1884 - 1894	John Offerman
1894 - 1900	Dennis Collins
with 1899 - 1922	Martin Brey (at Scarthingwell Hall)
1900 - 1910	Michael Bradley
1910 - 1922	Thomas Corcoran
1922 - 1937	Bernard McGurk
1937 - 1952	Thomas Corcoran
1952 - 1957	Jerome O'Sullivan
1957 - 1965	Augustine Forkin
1965 - 1969	Patrick Kelly
1969 - 1970	Robert McGregor
1970 - 1978	Francis Abberton
1978 - 1983	David Foskew
1983 - 1990	Paul Moxon

The Parish of St Joseph the Worker, Sherburn in Elmet

1990 - 1992	Gerald Creasey
1992 - 1994	Michael Lynch
1994 - 1997	David Massey
1997 - 2018	Michael McCarthy
2018 - 2019	Steven Billington
2019 - 2022	David Bulmer
2022 - 2023	Timothy Swinglehurst
2023 -	Henry Longbottom

Foreword by Father Paul F. Moxon
Parish Priest: 1983-1990

In the Old Testament, we are told that the Hebrews wandered in the wilderness for forty years as they made their way from Egypt to the promised land. For the people of Sherburn-in-Elmet it has not been quite so long in their search for a fitting place to worship, it has only seemed that long.

When I first came to the parish, a large dossier of letters and plans was handed to me. It contained the record of the tortuous journey that had been travelled since 1972 when the 'Sherburn Project' was first considered.

All that is behind us now and today we can look at our fine building in Sherburn and praise God that so much endeavour by priests and people in the past has at last come to fruition.

I said when I first came to the parish, that desirable as bricks and mortar were as an expression of our faith, and as a fitting place of worship, that it was primarily ourselves, as God's people, who had to be renewed and built up. The building must not be an end, but a beginning, and a means to evangelisation of ourselves and our community.

So we come to a new era; our parish continues to be dedicated to the Immaculate Conception and we must not lose our sense of belonging to a parish with a fine history. The Church at Sherburn-in-Elmet has been dedicated to St. Joseph the Worker on whose feast day the first sod was struck, but it is being completed in the month in which we celebrate our patronal feast of the Immaculate Conception. The Church at Scarthingwell, the first to be dedicated to Mary as the Immaculate Conception in this country in 1854, remains a fine testimony to the faith which has always been strong in this area. As your priest, I am very privileged to count the Venerable Nicholas Postgate as a predecessor in the area. All this history too is briefly described elsewhere in this brochure.

To the Diocesan Estate Agents Messrs. Oliver Kitchen and Flyn and particularly to Mr. Michael Buswell we owe a debt of gratitude for help and guidance; to Mr. Stephen Langtry-Langton, the Architect for his ever present help and assistance through many difficulties; to the men who translated his plans into reality and put up with my 'daft questions' and who work for Clayton Bowmore and the other contractors; and above all to our own beloved Bishop William for allowing himself to be persuaded that we should 'go ahead' when all strictly commercial considerations would have counselled against it. To them all I say in your name a very special word of thanks and the assurance of our prayers.

Finally I must pay tribute to you, the people of the parish, who have responded so magnificently during these last twelve months to so many demands upon you. All I can ask of you in the future is that you pray as well in St. Joseph the Worker Church as you have in other churches. It is your Church. I hope you will use it to advance in love and knowledge and praise of our gracious God and his Son Jesus Chris.

Reproduced from 'The Immaculate Conception and St Joseph the Worker - a booklet to celebrate the opening of the new church' - 22nd December 1984

Introduction

From the outside, the Church of St Joseph the Worker in Sherburn-in-Elmet, North Yorkshire, may not rank amongst the most architecturally significant churches. The humble red brick structure with its adjoining presbytery has no particular pretensions of grandeur and is unlikely to grace the pages of Pevsner's *Buildings of England* any time soon.

Yet, the church has, for the last forty years, been at the heart of the Roman Catholic community of the parish. It is a comparatively short history. However, the church's construction represents merely one stage in a much longer and ongoing journey.

This book began as a simple history of a building, but as more and more people kindly shared their stories, it became impossible to separate the bricks and mortar from the lives of those who built and worshipped within it. Similarly, this parish does not exist in isolation but has been shaped by events and the world around us.

This is not The history - definitive and absolute. Merely a history, woven from a collection of memories as witnessed by some of those who were there. To them, I would like to express my profound gratitude for helping to bring this history to life. As might be expected over the course of four decades, recollections were not always consistent. I have done my best to draw together differing accounts, as well as utilising documentary evidence from the church archives wherever possible. For any inaccuracies in retelling that remain, I can only apologise. Nevertheless, I hope readers will enjoy this narrative in the spirit in which it was intended.

The title of this book comes originally from the First Letter of Saint Peter, though it was specifically chosen as a link to the opening of the church. A note in the order of service reminded the people who attended forty years ago that:

It is an occasion for all those present to rededicate themselves to the service of the Lord as 'Living stones'.

The Church of St Joseph the Worker and its accompanying Church of the Immaculate Conception, Scarthingwell, are special places for me, as they are for many other people. Indeed, they are more than just buildings. These stones are the physical embodiment of the shared history and living faith of people of this parish.

Chris Whitwood - December 2024

Living Stones

*A history of the church, parish and people of
St Joseph the Worker, Sherburn-in-Elmet*

Chris Whitwood FRSA

. 1 .

The Promised Land

Then they cried to the Lord in their trouble, and he delivered them from their distress. - Psalm 107:6

Mounted on the wall just inside the entrance of the Church of St. Joseph the Worker, is a brass plaque commemorating the opening of the church. On Saturday 22nd December 1984, Roman Catholic parishioners of Sherburn-in-Elmet gathered for the blessing of their new place of worship with a Mass led by The Right Reverend William Gordon Wheeler, Bishop of Leeds.

The new church had been a long time coming to fruition. In the booklet produced to commemorate the occasion, parish priest Father Paul Moxon reflected on the sometimes arduous journey.

In the Old Testament we are told that the Hebrews wandered in the wilderness for forty years as they made their way from Egypt to the promised land. For the people of Sherburn-in-Elmet it has not been quite so long in their search for a fitting place to worship, it has only seemed that long.

Plans for a new church had begun over a decade before the first foundations were dug, during which time the community had to make do with the old cinema, intended only as a temporary chapel when it was purchased some eighteen years prior. Little wonder that the consecration of the Church of St. Joseph the Worker was welcomed as a new era with a sense of

Above: The plaque inside the entrance of the Church of St Joseph the Worker commemorating the opening.

Above: All Saints' Church, Sherburn-in-Elmet, in 1885.

joy and not a little relief. Yet, the church building is only the latest stage of a parish journey that stretches back much further.

Prior to the English Reformation, Christian life in Sherburn-in-Elmet centred around All Saints' church. However, Henry VIII's split from Rome divided Catholic from Protestant and triggered a wave of religious upheaval. This was part of a wider Reformation movement that was convulsing Europe but, being bound up with the king's personal and political troubles, it took on a distinctly English flavour. The monasteries were dissolved, and the great abbeys and priories that once dominated much of the country were devastated. Being a Catholic became a civil crime, being a priest was an act of treason, and harbouring one carried grave consequences.

There was resistance. In 1536, a popular uprising in Yorkshire, known as the Pilgrimage of Grace, spread across the North in defence of the 'Old Faith'. The Pilgrimage, along with similar revolts, was harshly suppressed. The leader, Robert Aske, was executed in York.

Above: Two views of Huddleston Hall. The present hall was built in the 16th century for the Hungate family, who were Lords of the Manor of Sherburn and continued to support Catholic worship.

Right: The 15th or 16th century chapel of Huddleston Hall.

There was brief respite for Catholics when 'Bloody' Mary I succeeded her brother, the no less bloody Edward VI. With the accession of Elizabeth I, a Protestant monarch returned to the throne. The reinstatement of the Acts of Supremacy and of Uniformity in 1559 once again placed the monarch at the head of the Church of England, made attendance of Anglican services compulsory, and prohibited by law all forms of Catholic worship. For much of the next three hundred years, Roman Catholics in England were penalised, prosecuted and persecuted for the profession of their faith.

The survival of Catholicism in this part of the Diocese of Leeds was due in no small part to a succession of priests and laity who continued to practise in spite of the legal restrictions placed upon Roman Catholics. Wealthy patrons were particularly important for ensuring Catholic centres endured. Diocesan archives reveal that such centres flourished at Saxton Hall, Huddleston Hall and Scarthingwell throughout the seventeenth and eighteenth century under the patronage of the Hungate, Hammond and, later, Gascoigne families.

Of the three halls only Huddleston survives. It is a fine Elizabethan manor house with locally quarried limestone walls the same dusty yellow as the late-summer wheat fields that roll into the distance. The medieval hall at Saxton was demolished in the early nineteenth century and Scarthingwell followed in the mid-twentieth.

One notable priest to have served the area was the Venerable Nicholas Postgate. He was ordained in 1628 having attended seminary in Douai, northern France, and returned to England two years later. While most homecoming priests landed on the south coast, Father Postgate returned to Yorkshire. On 29th June 1630, the feast of Saints Peter and Paul, he landed near Whitby where a safehouse awaited. He then made his way on foot to Saxton Hall to take up the position of Chaplain to Lady Hungate. He ministered to her for a decade until her death.

At this time Mass was said in secret and in later years, Father Postgate would often adopt the disguise of a gardener as he ministered to parishioners of his native Blackamoor, a vast parish in the North York Moors covering Guisborough, Scarborough and Pickering.

Right: A posthumous portrait of the Venerable Nicholas Postgate (circa 1710), now housed in the Whitby Museum.

The fabricated Popish Plot of 1678 led to a resurgence in anti-Catholic fear and persecution. The following year, the eighty-two year old Nicholas Postgate was arrested for being a priest and was executed on the Knavesmire in York - one of the Eighty-five martyrs of England and Wales beatified by Pope John Paul II.

With the systematic dismantling of the Catholic church hierarchy in England following the Reformation, it was necessary for a new structure to be established. By the end of the seventeenth century, this took the form of four Apostolic Vicariates - a missionary region overseen by a titular bishop.

The Northern District consisted of the historic counties of Cheshire, Lancashire, Cumberland, Westmorland, Northumberland, Durham, and Yorkshire, plus the Isle of Man. Huddleston Hall was at the heart of this new mission as it was the place of residence for the third Vicar Apostolic of the Northern District, Bishop Thomas Dominic Williams, until his death on 3rd April 1740.

Around the same period, Scarthingwell was also enduring as a Catholic centre thanks to the patronage of the Hammond family. Records from 1688 show that a priest was serving as chaplain to Mrs Hammond. He was followed by a succession of priests well into the next century. The family also supported other centres, including Saxton. However, when George Hammond, the last surviving member of the family, died in 1756, the estates passed to Edward Hawke. As First Lord of the Admiralty, Hawke was instrumental in the decision to approve James Cook's first voyage to Australia. Indeed, Hawke's Bay in New Zealand is named in his honour. However, his inheritance brought the use of Scarthingwell as a place of Catholic worship to a close.

This signalled a decline in the Catholic presence in the area. A priest, Father Hugh Franklin, ministered at Huddleston Hall in the 1750s, but by the end of the century, both Huddleston and Saxton Hall had also ceased to be places of worship. As a result, those wishing to hear Mass had to travel either to Hazelwood or Aberford, where nearby Parlington Hall was the seat of the devout Gascoigne family.

Throughout the seventeenth and eighteenth centuries the Gascoignes contributed to funds that brought Benedictine priests over from France. The marriage of Sir Edward Gascoigne to Mary Hungate in 1726 brought two of the main Catholic families in the area together. When Sir Charles Carrington Hungate, the last male of that name, died in 1749, the estates were merged - not that the new owners were present to enjoy their inheritance. Sir Edward had travelled extensively in his youth, spending thirteen years (1713-1726) on a Grand Tour of Europe, as was the fashion for wealthy young men of the era. However, in May 1743 he left England once more, this time taking his family with him to live in Cambrai, northern France.

The reason for the departure has never been fully explained. Sir Edward's diary entries hint that his wife's ill-health or a wish to be near his sisters, who were nuns at a convent in Cambrai, are possible explanations. Yet, the political situation for Catholics was also precarious. Catholics were required to register their names and additional taxes were levied against them, such as the 1722 'papists tax' and a double land tax for Catholic property owners. The deposition of James II and subsequent rebellions attempting to restore the Stuart monarchy had become a cause célèbre, culminating in the Jacobite Rising of 1745. In such a fevered atmosphere, Catholic nobles, such as the Gascoignes, would be particularly vulnerable if they fell out of political favour.

The journey from Parlington Hall to Cambrai by coach and ship would have taken at least a week, and likely much more. The fact that the couple's second son (also called Edward) was scarcely three-months old when the journey was made suggests a degree of urgency. Whatever the reason, neither Sir Edward nor his newborn son would see Parlington again. It was not until 1763 that Sir Edward and Mary's third son, Thomas (their first son, John Francis, had died young), returned to Parlington, and then only for a brief visit.

Like his father, Sir Thomas was a frequent traveller and spent much time on the continent with his friend, the writer Henry Swinburne. As well-connected Catholics, the pair gained access to the leading courts of Europe and spent time with many prominent figures, including King Charles III of Spain, King Ferdinand I of the Two Sicilies and Pope Pius VI. His travels also brought him into contact with Enlightenment ideas. He became an ardent supporter of American Independence, ordering the erection of a triumphal arch, which can still be visited on the Partlington estate.

On his return to England in 1780, Sir Thomas renounced 'the errors of the Church of Rome' in the presence of the Archbishop of Canterbury. This was most likely a pragmatic move to allow him to take up a seat in Parliament rather than being driven by religious conviction. Indeed, despite his public conversion, he allowed the priest to continue to live in the church on his estate, and financed the construction of St. Wilfrid's in Aberford, where Mass would continue to be said until the church's deconsecration in 1991.

While wealthy Catholics may have been able to escape to enjoy the hospitality of the European nobility, the majority of ordinary lay Catholics were still subject to civil and political restrictions. Threat of execution had waned but recusancy (refusal to attend Church of England services) was still punishable by fines. A year after the 1715 Jacobite rebellion, there were three-hundred and fifty convictions in the North Riding of Yorkshire alone. Mass was still said in private in country-house chapels and worshippers from Sherburn-in-Elmet and South Milford had to travel several miles in order to receive Communion. It was not until 1791 that Catholics in England would finally be granted freedom of worship.

Left: Sir Thomas Gascoigne (1745–1810), 8th Baronet of Parlington Hall. Painted by Pompeo Batoni in 1779.

Below: St Wilfrid's in Aberford, now a private residence. Note the large semi-circular church windows on the left hand side of the building.

The middle decades of the nineteenth century saw a Roman Catholic resurgence. With the passing of the Catholic Emancipation Act in 1829, Catholics gained the right to sit as Members of Parliament and take up all but a handful of public offices. The Oxford Movement, which developed amongst high-church members of the Church of England, sought a renewal of some older Christian traditions and prompted the conversion of many leading thinkers, including Saint John Henry Newman, to Catholicism.

Significant immigration from Ireland in the century that followed helped swell congregations but also, in some areas, fuelled divisions between incoming Catholics and English protestants.

A 'second spring' of Catholicism in England was heralded in 1850 when Pope Pius IX issued a papal bull, Universalis Ecclesiae, re-establishing the Roman diocesan hierarchy in England. A backlash against perceived 'Papal aggression' resulted in a short-lived Act of Parliament attempting to prohibit the use of English ecclesiastical titles by Catholic bishops, and while the Act was repealed in 1871, the names adopted for the new Catholic dioceses were intentionally different from the existing Anglican ones.

In Scarthingwell, this spring came with the arrival of the Maxwell family in 1850. The Maxwells were a Scottish family with links to Herries baronetcy and the deposed Stuart monarchy. Their ancestral home of Traquair House, about twenty-five miles south of Edinburgh and now a country-house bed and breakfast, is claimed to be the oldest continually inhabited house in Scotland.

For the first four years after the Maxwell family's arrival, parishioners attended Mass in the private chapel of Scarthingwell Hall. A mid-seventeenth century building, on

Above: Watercolour painting of Scarthingwell Hall and adjoining church by Laura Wilson Taylor (née Barker) dated 'Sep 9 1875'. The entrance to the church is no longer visible from this angle due to the 1950s extension.

(Image credit: www.artwarefineart.com)

Below: Photograph of Scarthingwell Hall taken in 1930. The west end of the church can be seen on the right.

the site of an old maltings for Kirkstall Abbey and located on London Road just outside Barkston Ash, was purchased for use as a presbytery. Priests serving the parish resided here from 1852 until construction of a new presbytery as part of the Church of St Joseph the Worker in 1984.

In 1854, Henry Constable Maxwell donated some four thousand pounds, a considerable sum at the time, for the construction of the present church at Scarthingwell, which originally adjoined the Hall.

The church is Italian late-Romanesque in style, chosen to complement the hall. The restrained exterior of Huddleston limestone and slate roof belies the lavish plasterwork inside. The ornately stencilled vaulted apse is divided into seven segments, beneath each of which is a tall, slim stained-glass window. Where these segments meet in the ceiling's dome is carved a dove, born aloft on outstretched wings.

Above: The Church of the Immaculate Conception and St John of Beverley, Scarthingwell.

Above: The exquisitely painted vaulted apse ceiling above the altar.

Below: The seven stained glass windows illuminating the east end of the church.

At the east end of the church stands the delicately carved high altar decorated with a lamb, flanked by representations of the Sacred Heart on either side. The tabernacle is adorned with two angels, one of which was damaged by burglars in the late-1990s. Unfortunately, restoration work was unable to disguise the fact that the wings of one angel are now shorter than those on the other.

Four windows of clear glass, in round-headed arches characteristic of the Romanesque style, line the nave. From between each window, leaps a semi-circular arch supporting the roof. The decorated floral plasterwork of acanthus and vine scroll echoes the floor of red, black and yellow patterned encaustic tiles. The numbered loose pews are original.

The gallery, which can now only be accessed by a narrow, wooden spiral staircase opposite the main entrance, was almost certainly designed as a family pew for the Maxwell-Stewarts. The Charles Allen organ situated in the loft dates from the church's opening in 1854 and is highly regarded as an unrestored instrument of the period.

Left: The organ loft and original Charles Allen organ, which is accessed through a door below the loft and up a set of narrow stairs on the right of the image.

Left: The Lamb of God surrounded by vine leaves in the centre of the high altar.

Right: West end of the church, which was previously connected to Scarthingwell Hall.

Below: The angels standing on top of the tabernacle. The one on the left has shorter wings than the one on the right.

The west end of the church has been subject to most change. The entrance from the house was blocked in 1956 after Scarthingwell Hall was demolished and the present front, incorporating a single bell tower on the south west corner, was constructed. Nevertheless, the majority of the church remains much as it would have appeared when it was first built.

The opening was a grand affair. High Mass, lasting two and a half hours, was celebrated by an assembly of nearly fifty priests, among whom were Cardinal Nicholas Wiseman, the first Archbishop of Westminster; the Right Reverend John Briggs, Bishop of the Diocese of Beverley, which at that time covered almost the whole of Yorkshire; and many members of the Catholic nobility and gentry of the county. The church was jointly dedicated to the Immaculate Conception (the first church in England to bear this name) and St John of Beverley. A wellingtonia, giant redwood tree, was planted in the park to commemorate the occasion. For the first time in nearly three centuries, Catholics in Barkston Ash, Sherburn-in-Elmet, and the surrounding area had their own parish church in which they could freely worship.

The first priest to serve the new parish of Scarthingwell was the Reverend Charles Augustus O'Neil and it was during his time that the school in Barkston Ash was built, again funded by the Maxwell family for the cost of £229 and 9 shillings. The school has been altered substantially over the years but the original building remains. The self-contained teacher's flat on the upper floor has since been converted into classrooms.

Above: Barkston Ash Catholic Primary School. Extensions have been added over the years, but the original, two-storey brick building paid for by the Maxwell family is still plainly visible.

Below: Pupils of Barkston Ash school in 1913, possibly at a presentation of the Good Attendance Shield. Father Brey is stood in the centre at the back.

By 1890, the number of parishioners at Scarthingwell had grown to between 350 and 400. The fortunes of the Maxwell family had also increased. The death of Lady Louisa Stuart of Traquair in her one-hundredth year meant the Scottish seat passed to Henry Constable Maxwell. Acutely aware of Traquair's history and his own family's connections, he added the Stuart surname to his own.

The Maxwell-Stuart family remained at Scarthingwell ensuring there was not only a priest to serve the parish but also a chaplain to minister to the spiritual welfare of the family. For the first two decades of the twentieth century, the role was fulfilled by Father Martin Brey, a tall, austere-looking Dutch priest who had previously served in Batley and Pontefract. Meanwhile, Father Michael Bradley and later Father Thomas Corcoran attended to the needs of the parish.

This arrangement would last until Father Brey's retirement on the grounds of ill health in 1922, after which Father Bernard McGurk succeeded Father Corcoran as priest, serving both the parish and the Maxwell-Stuarts. The tranquil solitude of Scarthingwell, set amid the wooded parkland overlooking the lake laid out by John Davenport at the instruction of the Hawke family in the early 1790s, must have held a particular draw as Father Corcoran returned in 1937. He remained a further fifteen years until his retirement, having served the parish a total of twenty-seven years - the longest of any priest to date.

It was during this time that George, the last surviving child of Henry Constable Maxwell-Stuart, died. The Scarthingwell estates, including the hall, church, presbytery and school were bequeathed to the Diocese of Leeds. For a short while, a community of nuns of the Order of Saint Clare (Poor Clare Sisters) took up residence in the hall but left in 1954, after which it remained empty. By 1960, Scarthingwell Hall had fallen into a state of disrepair and, though the church remained, the rest of the building was demolished. In its place, a school, dedicated to St Camillus, was constructed.

§ § §

The eyes of most visitors to Scarthingwell Church would almost certainly be drawn to the stained-glass windows illuminating the altar or the exquisitely painted roof above. Few would take time to closely examine the seats of the pews in any great detail. Those who do may notice evidence of graffiti made by former pupils. Ink stains, letters scratched into the wood or paler patches where the graffiti, and with it the wood's original dark staining, has been sanded away, are testimony to the boys' mandatory attendance at Mass.

Above: Graffiti on the pews at Scarthingwell, possibly made by boys of St Camillus' school.

St Camillus' Approved School for Roman Catholic Senior Boys was a residential behavioural institution run by the Leeds Catholic Child Welfare Society. It could accommodate up to thirty boys between the ages of fifteen and seventeen years, along with housing for teachers and staff. In 1973, following the abolition of the Approved Schools system, the school became a Community Home with Education (CHE) under the control of West Riding of Yorkshire County Council. It remained so until it closed ten years later. It is a source of great pain that the memory of St Camillus' School has been marred by the subsequent conviction of former staff members for abuse of pupils.

After the school closed, the premises were converted for use as a care home for the elderly. A new, purpose-built facility was completed in 2024 and is occupied by Highfield Care Home, providing residential and dementia care.

§ § §

For Roman Catholics in England, the four hundred years following King Henry VIII's break with Rome was a story of trial, survival and ultimately rebirth. This history gave Catholicism in England a distinctive character when compared with other parts of Europe where the faith had remained the dominant force.

The collective memory of a time when Roman Catholics were the oppressed, has the potential to lead to a deepened understanding of injustice and religious intolerance. It may also be reflected in a desire to reach across ecumenical divides in search of Christian unity, while at the same time strengthening faith and a sense of Catholic identity in an increasingly secular world.

After all, it was the obstinate conviction of Catholics such as Nicholas Postgate, rather than the pragmatism of men like Thomas Gascoigne, that guaranteed the survival of the Faith in England during the centuries of persecution.

Nevertheless, for all the generosity of patrons and the courage of missionaries and martyrs, Roman Catholicism could not have endured without also the quiet faith of lay parishioners whose names do not feature in the history books.

In many ways, this balance between an active profession of faith, private prayer and public pragmatism remains relevant to many modern Catholics. The strength and certainty of the saints may sometimes be hard to find, yet inspiration can still be taken from those who have gone before.

. 2 .

Foundations

Rejoice in hope, be patient in suffering, persevere in prayer. - Romans 12:12

1952 was a year of new beginnings. The death of King George VI saw his twenty-five year old daughter accede to the throne, heralding what some at the time described as a second Elizabethan age. A seventeen-year old Elvis Presley, started his final year in high school and decided his future lay in music. Dwight D. Eisenhower became the first Republican elected to the White House in nearly a quarter of a century; on the other side of the world, India held its first elections since independence; and in post-war Europe, the Coal and Steel Community came into being.

On a more local level for the Catholic parishioners of Scarthingwell, this was also the year when Father Thomas Corcoran finally retired and was succeeded as parish priest by Father Jerome O'Sullivan. Sherburn-in-Elmet had grown in size and importance over the previous years and Father O'Sullivan soon realised that somewhere less remote was required to meet the needs of those in the south of the parish. For those travelling on foot, the almost four mile walk from South Milford would take well over an hour. The location he lighted on was the Blackburn Aircraft Corporation Hostel on Moor Lane.

The Blackburn Aircraft company was founded by Robert Blackburn in 1914 and during the Second World War achieved the feat of manufacturing 1,699 Fairey Swordfish (torpedo

Above: Avery Scales factory, previously owned by the Blackburn Aircraft Corporation.

armed naval biplanes, perhaps most famous for their role in sinking the German battleship *Bismarck*) in just three years. As was the case in many other industries, a hostel was established near the factory to accommodate workers relocated to meet the demands of wartime production. This was a modest location for a religious service but nonetheless significant. When weekly Mass was first said in 1955, it became the first regular place of Catholic worship in Sherburn itself.

Right: Looking up the High Street from the crossroads. The roof of the Old Courthouse can be made out over the crest of Finkle Hill.

Below: Troops marching past the courthouse and police station (about 1918).

The end of the war had brought with it a significant reduction in demand for military aircraft and by the time Masses began in the hostel, Blackburn had already moved production to Brough and Avery Scales had taken over the Sherburn factory. The hostel remained the Mass centre for the village's Catholic community until 1963.

A short-term solution, closer to the centre of the village, was found in the Old Courthouse building on Finkle Hill - now the site of the police station. Each Sunday, seats and an altar table were set out in the cold, green-painted room where Mass was said, before having to be tidied away again afterwards. For three years, this arrangement sufficed but it was far from ideal.

§ § §

The parishioners of Sherburn-in-Elmet may only have worshipped in the courthouse for a short time, but it was during these years that a thousand miles away in Rome, one of the most important events in the history of the Church unfolded. The ramifications would be felt by Catholics worldwide.

On 11th October 1962, about 2,400 bishops from across the world, accompanied by 500 theologians, gathered to convene

Left: Pope Saint John XXIII.

Right top: Before a papal Mass in St Peter's Basilica during the Second Vatican Council.
(Image credit: Lothar Wolleh, CC 3.0)

Right bottom: Bishops gather in St Peter's Square (1962).

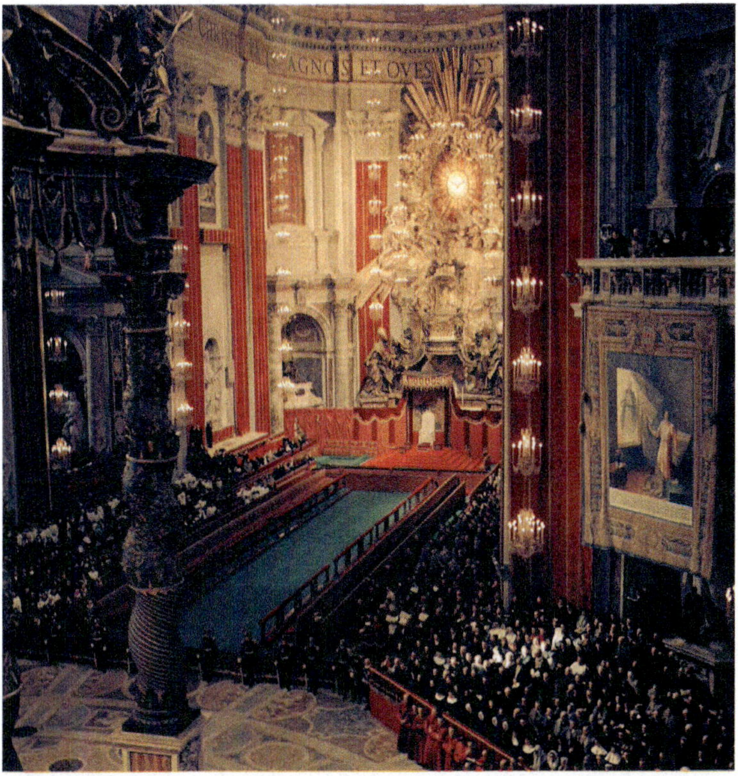

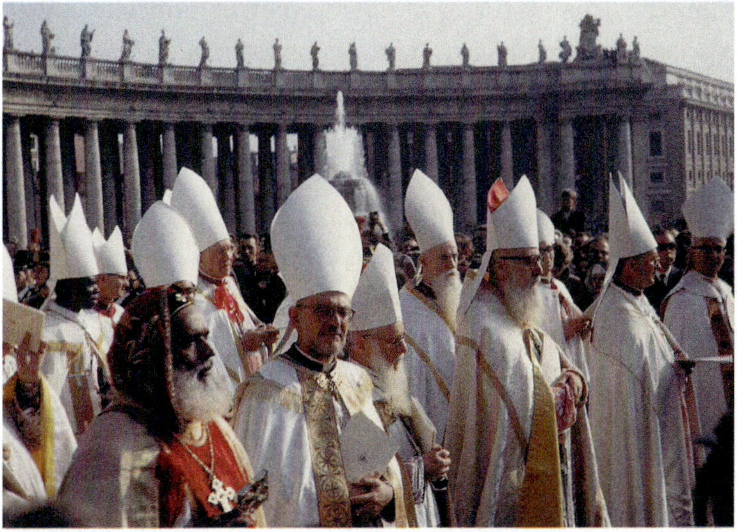

the Second Ecumenical Council of the Vatican, commonly referred to simply as Vatican II. The Counter Reformation of the sixteenth and early seventeenth centuries redefined the teachings of the Catholic Church. The Council of Trent refuted what it saw as protestant heresies and positioned the Church as separate from the outside world. For four hundred years, the Church remained in lockdown and resistant to change.

Pope Saint John XXIII sought to address this and bring about 'the growth of the Catholic faith, the restoration of sound morals among the Christian flock, and appropriate adaptation of Church discipline to the needs and conditions of our times'.[1] The word he used to describe this was *Aggiornamento*, literally 'bringing up to date' but that goes nowhere near to expressing the scope and profundity of what he had in mind. His vision was of 'a new Pentecost' to 'open the windows' and let the Holy Spirit blow through the Church.

While often viewed as an attempt at liberal modernisation, the ambition at the heart of the Council might more accurately be defined as a desire to recapture the essential tradition of the Church. This idea is expressed in another principle closely associated with Vatican II: *Ressourcement*, meaning 'return to the sources'. Over the previous century, rediscovery and study of historic Church documents led to the realisation that a divergence had occurred between the early Church and the Church at the time of the Council.

In response, some of the reforms following the Second Vatican Council sought to restore some Early Church liturgical traditions, such as the Sign of Peace, whilst at the same time eliminating other practices that were believed to originate from the Middle Ages.

---

1. *Ad Petri Cathedram - Encyclical of Pope John XIII on Truth, Unity and Peace, in a Spirit of Charity (1959)*

An important element of the Council's vision was to encourage the Faithful's 'full and active participation' in liturgical celebrations.[2] If *Aggiornamento* was to bring the Church up to date, it could only be achieved by a greater common understanding of the teachings of Christ and knowledge of Scripture and the Liturgy. The revised Mass thus contains more scriptural readings than the pre-Council Mass. Greater use of the vernacular - the language of the people - was permitted and encouraged where appropriate. The lay faithful were called to a new vocation founded on a deepening of faith and 'a strengthened sense of personal responsibility'.[3]

An architectural expression of the liturgical reforms resulting from the Second Vatican Council can be seen in the different positions of the altars in Scarthingwell and Sherburn. Whereas the altar in Scarthingwell is placed immediately below the Tabernacle in the east end of the sanctuary so that the priest celebrates the Mass 'ad orientem' (eastern-facing), in Sherburn the altar is free-standing which enables the priest to celebrate the Mass 'versus populum' (facing the People). Another feature flowing out of the post Vatican Council liturgical reforms is the position of the ambo (also known as the lectern) in the sanctuary. In the original Scarthingwell church there would not have been a permanent ambo from which the biblical readings were delivered. Instead, a movable stand would have been used from which only the priest would read. By contrast, in St Joseph's the ambo is a stationary feature integral to the overall design of the sanctuary representing the two important aspects of the Mass: Word and Eucharist.

§ § §

---

2. *Sacrosanctum Concilium - Constitution on the Sacred Liturgy (1963)*
3. *Lumen Gentium - Dogmatic Constitution on the Church (1964)*

While the Council was taking place in Rome, parish life continued and the practical, everyday concerns remained. Still in search of a more permanent place of worship, it came to the notice of Father O'Sullivan's successor, Father Augustine Forkin, that the old cinema on Low Street was up for sale. He set the wheels in motion for the building to be purchased.

The site had originally been a maltings for Sherburn's windmill. While the old cellars remained, the building had been converted by the time a fire ripped through the mill in November 1921. As the flames spread, the sails broke loose and began to turn, spraying cinders high into the afternoon sky and creating a blazing beacon that could be seen for miles around. The desperate efforts of the fire brigade were not enough to save the mill but the adjacent cinema was spared.

Above: Sherburn windmill before and after the fire. The low building beside it would become the cinema and later the Catholic chapel.

Right: 'Qualter for Quality' - stalls outside the Qualter's shop.

The 'Cinema: Sherburn-in-Elmet', often referred to as 'Sherburn Pictures', started small with only a couple of screenings a week. Yet, business grew and soon films were being shown every night, with a double bill on Saturdays. Films were not the only entertainment on offer. The cinema also played host to dances and wartime fundraising events. However, by the 1960s, the heyday of cinema had passed and the seats in the picturehouse became harder to fill. The Mills family, who had been long-time owners, saw which way the wind was blowing. The cinema was acquired by David Booth, but eventually he too resigned himself to the inevitable. The cinema closed and the building was put up for sale.

As a sizable, single-storey building able to comfortably accommodate large gatherings, it seemed the perfect answer, at least temporarily, to the prayers of Sherburn's Catholic community. An additional parcel of land behind the building - leased by the Qualter family, owners of the large farm shop on Low Street - would subsequently prove an invaluable asset.

Father Forkin left the parish before the purchase of the cinema was complete. Nevertheless, the year after his departure, an enthusiastic band of volunteers, led by their new priest Father Patrick Kelly, set about the task of converting it from leisure to liturgical use. It was perhaps in recognition of their efforts that, in January 1967, the new chapel was dedicated to St Joseph the Worker in the parish of Scarthingwell. It was a humble chapel, but when all was said and done the lay people of Sherburn had taken their strengthened sense of personal responsibility upon their shoulders and built for themselves a church.

Father Kelly remained for a further two years, while the parishioners in Sherburn settled into their new place of worship. His departure in 1969 was followed by a brief interlude, during which the parish was briefly served by Father Robert McGregor, before he too was replaced, in 1970, by Father Francis Abberton. It was under his pastoral leadership that the idea for a new church first began to be explored. For the first six years, limited headway was made so, with Father Abberton's retirement, the mantle of developing the project passed to the parish's next priest.

§ § §

Father David Foskew was in every sense a gentle man. His quiet kindness is remembered fondly by his former housekeeper, Margaret Holt (now Addyman).

She had initially agreed to take on the role of housekeeper for only four weeks, but after that time had elapsed and she asked if he had found a replacement, Father Foskew confessed he had yet to start looking. She would remain with him for the next four years.

Above: Father Foskew with First Holy Communion children alongside Marian Bolton, who prepared the children, and Donald Foster, head of Barkston Ash school.

    The son of a railwayman and a school dinner lady, Father Foskew came from a background that was, if not similar, at least relatable to many parishioners. Having achieved the rank of Major as a chaplain in the territorial army, Father Foskew learned a common touch that made him approachable to soldier and parishioner alike.

    Margaret soon learned that a top tip for any priest's housekeeper was to keep a ready amount of dog collars in her coat pocket should the need for an impromptu blessing arise and the request, 'Quick, pass me a collar.', was uttered. The source of such a plentiful supply, however, came not from the divine but from white, washing up liquid bottles, carefully cut into strips and handed to Father Foskew with a reminder to make sure he put it on the right way round so as to avoid the risk of having the word 'Fairy' written on his neck.

The development of a new church for Sherburn-in-Elmet continued little by little. Margaret would set out plans on the dining table for Father Foskew to study and take phone calls from the architect firm, J. H. Langtry-Langton, keen to know whether their client had had chance to give the latest scheme consideration.

Designs were drawn and redrawn. Letters were sent. Thought was given to how it all might be afforded. All the while, parish life at Scarthingwell, the school in Barkston Ash and the chapel in Sherburn-in-Elmet continued.

Of course, a priest only serves a parish at the behest of the bishop, and in Bishop Wheeler's summer moves in 1983, Father Foskew was appointed to the parish of St Joseph in Barnoldswick. It is a sign of the affection that parishioners felt for him that a trip to Barnoldswick was organised in June 1988 on the occasion of his jubilee to celebrate Mass in his new church and enjoy a social event with members of the congregation there.

This was an affection he clearly shared. On the eve of his departure, Father Foskew said simply to his devoted housekeeper, Margaret,

'I don't want to go.'

These words are all the more poignant as shortly after moving, he was diagnosed with throat cancer. On 2nd October 1988, Father David Foskew died at the age of only forty-nine.

§ § §

When Father Foskew's replacement, Father Paul Moxon, arrived in the parish, he found he had quite the task on his hands. The presbytery had, what an estate agent might euphemistically term, 'potential'. What it also had, as Father Moxon was to discover in his first winter at the parish, was a severe heating problem. The large building had been divided in two, with one part as living quarters and the other used for storing old furniture. Thick stone walls kept the building cold during the summer and an inefficient wood-fired boiler did little to warm the inhabited half during the winter - although this situation was ever so slightly improved when it was discovered that the boiler was actually supposed to run on coal.

Even in Father Foskew's time the residence had been deemed unsuitable for an older priest and by January 1984 it was not only cold, damp and draughty, but also in need of substantial repair.

Father Moxon also inherited one of his predecessor's two cats. Father Foskew had taken the tom with him but left the female feline to live a semi-feral existence, only returning to the presbytery to have kittens and leave the new priest wondering how best to avoid being overrun with cats.

The siting of the presbytery was also far from ideal. It was not within easy walking distance of either the church in Scarthingwell or the old cinema chapel in Sherburn, and the isolated location made it prone to burglaries. Writing in 1981, Father Foskew reported that it had been broken into four times the previous winter alone. The proximity of St Camillus school may have been a factor. One particularly unpleasant break-in, suspected though never proven to have been by residential pupils, had seen the culprits not only make off with a Parker pen and a pair of silver cufflinks, but also relieve themselves in Father Foskew's wardrobe.

It may have seemed easy for petty criminals to find the Presbytery but many parishioners did not know where it was, let alone visited it. The unsatisfactory situation was bluntly summed up by Father Moxon, who reported to the diocesan Financial Commission that the people in Sherburn 'are not well serviced by a priest living three miles away in a field'.

The state of the old cinema was not much better. It was accessed by a narrow track, which ran between the shops and the Elmete Social Club on Low Street, to a parking area separated from the social club by a stone wall. At the end of the car park ran a fence with a gate leading into the field that would eventually become the site of the new church.

The entrance from the car park led initially into a large porch, which even long after the cinema closed was still adorned with posters advertising long out-of-date film showings. From here, double doors opened into the main hall of the chapel. Immediately to the left was the organ, played during Mass by Mrs Roberts. Looking down the central aisle there was, to the left of the altar, a small sacristy - little more than a cubby hole. The altar itself stood just in front of where the cinema screen had been, giving the chapel the unusual quality of facing west, rather than east towards the rising sun - not that there was any natural light by which one would notice. The hall was windowless; its lighting, rudimentary. There were toilet facilities but even during the building's time as a cinema, these were remembered as being badly lit, if at all. Little had improved.

Having originally been built to store grain, the insulation was minimal. In winter, the only heating came from an industrial heater, generously provided by Bernard Qualter. While this could produce a significant amount of warmth, it also ran with the quietness and finesse of a jumbo jet engine

Above: The cinema chapel during its eventual demolition in the mid-1980s. The shops on Low Street are in the background.

Below: Inside the partially demolished chapel looking from the altar end towards the congregation. The window of the projector room, also visible in the top photograph, can be seen in the back wall.

meaning it was necessary to turn it off before Mass started if there was to be any hope of the Liturgy being heard. Meanwhile, the congregation shivered.

The old cinema chairs had been replaced by bench pews, behind which was enough space for a few tables to be set out for the Saturday school. Run by Bernard Whalley, his wife, Janet, and Marian Bolton, the Saturday school was created to provide children in the parish, who did not go to a faith school, with a Catholic education. Bernard had initially trained to be a priest himself at Ushaw College in County Durham, but left the seminary and shortly after, met Janet at a mutual friend's wedding. They married and moved to the parish where he became an RE teacher at St Wilfrid's Catholic High School in Featherstone and she taught at the primary school in Barkston Ash, along with Marian Bolton.

Such activities were typical of the close-knit parish community that existed at that time. Several parishioners had young families and it was hoped that as the village grew, so too would the congregation, but if that was going to happen, they needed a place fit for worship.

In late February 1982, Monsignor John Murphy, recently appointed Vicar General of the Diocese of Leeds, was dispatched by the Bishop to view the situation for himself. His assessment was damning. The chapel he described, bluntly, was a 'shack' and concluded 'the only treatment of which it is worthy is demolition'.

A new church was badly needed.

. 3 .

Perseverance

For which of you, intending to build a tower, does not first sit down and estimate the cost, to see whether he has enough to complete it? - Luke 14:28

The Roman architect Vitruvius, writing in the first century BC, stated that all buildings should possess the three attributes of *firmitas*, *utilitas*, and *venustas* (strength, utility, and beauty). The architect's notes on the church and presbytery plans for St Joseph the Worker admits that J. H. Langtry-Langton took an approach 'somewhat different from the old architectural adage', instead pursuing the principles of *cost*, *design* and *durability*.

To these maxims might also be added the virtue of perseverance. Langtry-Langton had first been approached to draw up designs in 1973 - the same year that the first application for outline planning permission was made to Tadcaster Rural District Council.

The intention was for a combined church and presbytery, built in the field behind the cinema, meaning the chapel could remain in use while construction of the new church was under way. The appearance in these early plans bore many similarities to what would eventually be constructed. A central porch would join the two parts of the building: to the left, the presbytery, and to the right, church.

The chief difference between aspiration and reality is the intention to have a large parish hall directly behind the church and running perpendicular to it. One entrance to the hall would have been from the back of the building. According to proposals described in the Catholic Building Review, a folding screen between the hall and the church itself could also be opened to make the space available for extra congregation when required.

The size of the church as originally intended by Father Abberton was, at least in Father Foskew's eyes, both excessive for the parish and too expensive for the challenging economic climate of the time. A prefabricated system building was considered, but as none of the available options were deemed suitable by Father Foskew for the desired purpose and needs of the parish in Sherburn, Langtry-Langton were approached to draw up new plans.

The design they came up with was for a presbytery, and a dual-purpose church and hall. This was to be built in such a

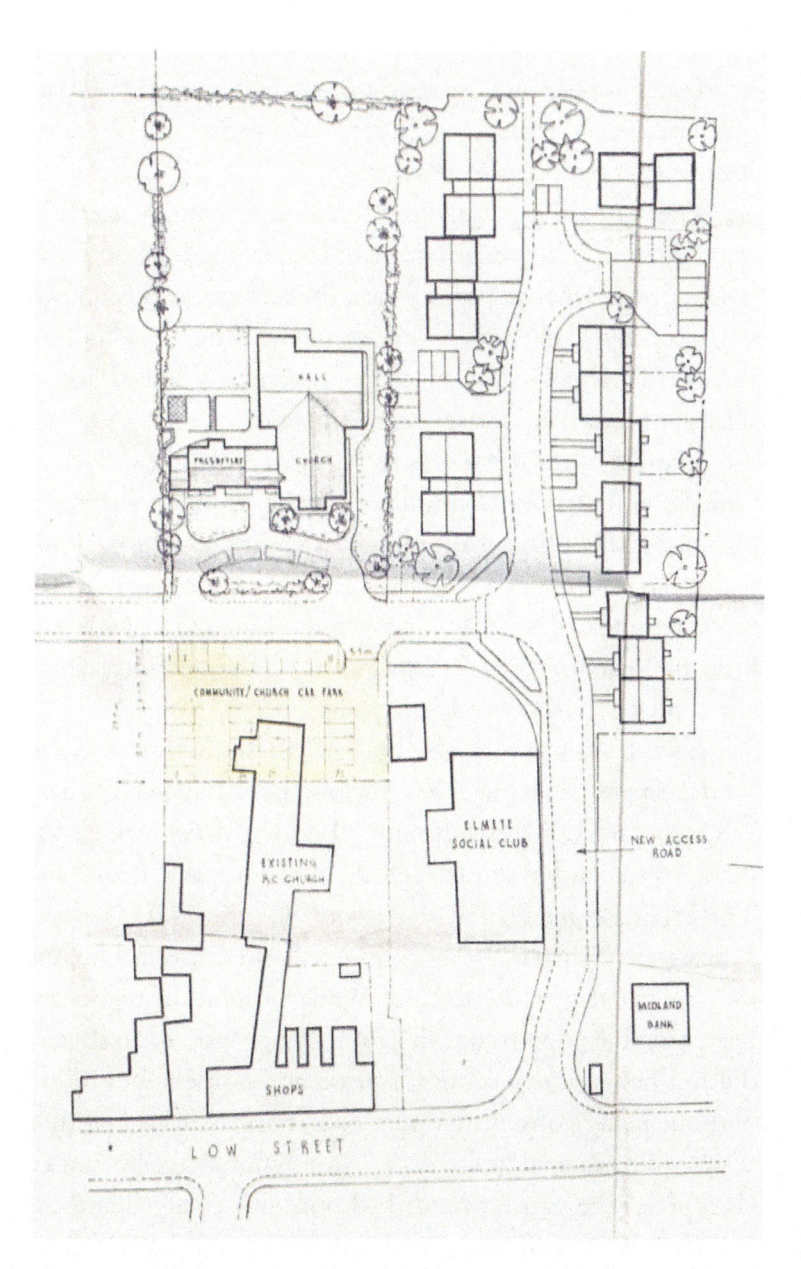

Above: Plan showing the early ambition for a church with a parish hall to the rear. The location of the cinema chapel is labelled as 'Existing RC Church'.

way that if it became feasible in future years, the existing part could become a permanent church and a parish hall be added at the rear as per previous designs.

The idea of just building a dedicated church was also explored. Given the active nature of the parish at the time and absence of alternative parish space, the collective decision was that a combined church and hall would be better. The 'Future Parish Hall' remained on subsequent plans as a dashed line in the hope of a second phase of development.

The new presbytery was to be in the form of a dormer bungalow. A standard bungalow had initially been suggested by the Bishop but, in a report written at the end of 1981, Father Foskew explained that 'when we got down to width measurements a dormer bungalow was more suitable with very little difference in cost'. This arrangement 'though not palatial' was thought to be perfectly adequate.

By the early 1980s, the time of priests having a live-in housekeeper was passing. Nevertheless, the plan dated February 1982, contained three bedrooms, one for a parish priest, one for a visitor and a third labelled 'Housekeeper's Bedroom'. The driving force behind this layout was the Vicar General, Monsignor Murphy, who considered Sherburn-in-Elmet a pleasant parish in which to retire. While the location might have been suitable, upon consideration the proposed presbytery did not have enough room for priest and housekeeper to live without being constantly under one another's feet. Hardly a recipe for peaceful retirement. Monsignor Murphy settled elsewhere. The parish priest's bedroom was enlarged and the housekeeper's room was set aside as the guest bedroom instead.

According to this plan, the downstairs of the presbytery was to be centred around a hall with a dining room to the right, which ran through to the sacristy and on to the church.

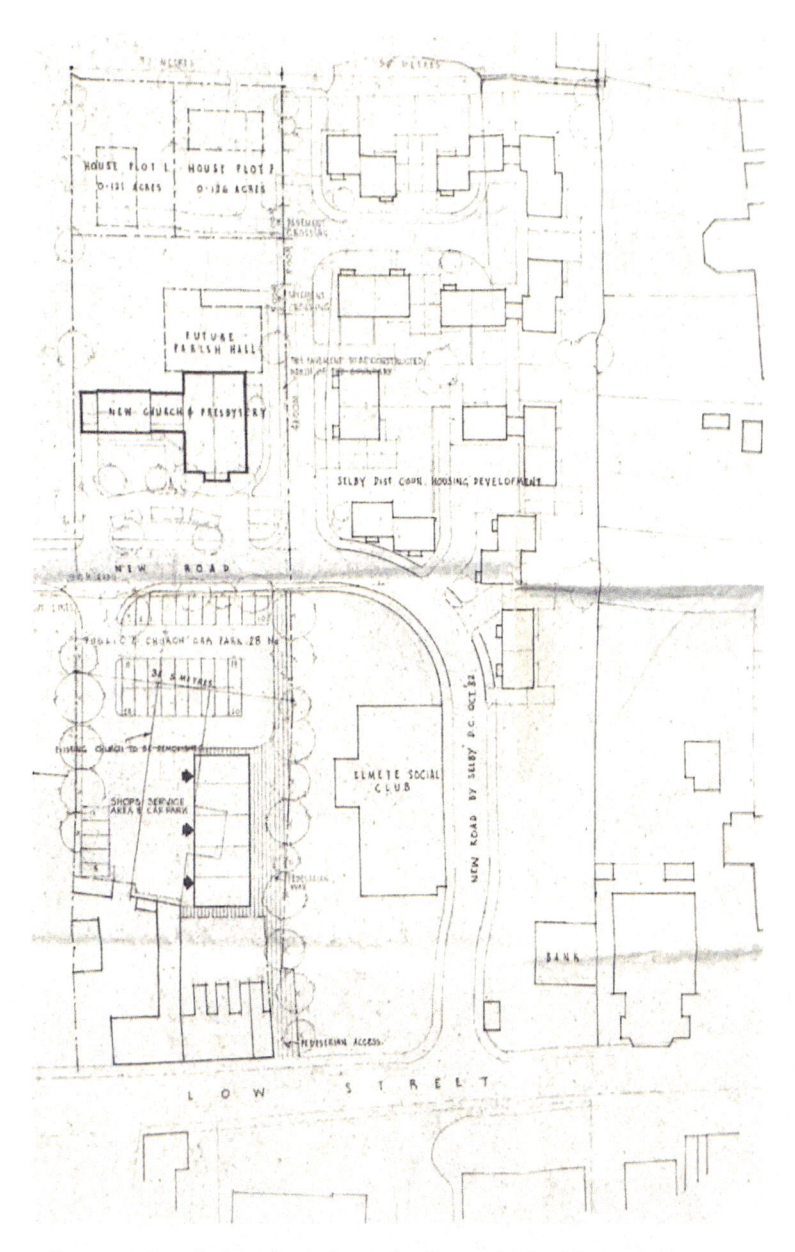

Above: Updated plans (March 1982). The parish hall is marked as a dashed line – an ambition for the future. Possible houses behind the church and shops on the site of the old cinema are also shown.

Immediately inside the door between the church and the sacristy was drawn a partition wall with a grate for confessions. On one side, a chair for the priest to hear the confession. On the other, there was space for a kneeler, although the inconvenient positioning of this would have meant that the confessor's feet would have obstructed the door.

Those attending Mass would have been greeted with an excess of doors. The main entrance was to be through a double door into a small, square foyer with space for tables on either side and large, recessed door mat. Then through another set of double doors into an 'Entrance Porch' or narthex. As on earlier designs, this section linked the presbytery and church.

From the porch, there would be two entrances into the church: a single door directly opposite the sacristy (presumably

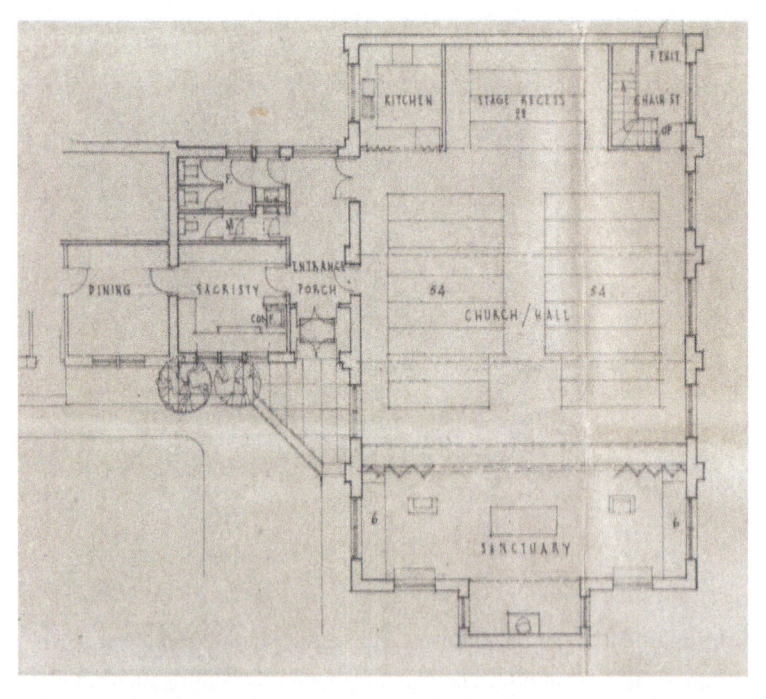

Above: An excess of doors. Plan of the Church/Hall (February 1982).

for use by the priest and altar servers) and a double door only a little way further along the same wall. At the end of the porch to the left were to be three toilets - one male and two female - each of which was reached by no fewer than three doors.

On entering the church/hall through the double doors, there was to be a kitchen on the left hand side. A folding shutter, facing in the direction of the altar, would open above a counter, which would have lifted bar-style to allow access to the kitchen itself. Next to the kitchen was space for a stage so that the chairs could be turned around and the hall used for events, such as school productions. In the back corner of the church furthest from the entrance was another door which would have led to a store, through which was a fire escape, and stairs up to the choir gallery situated above the stage area.

The church itself was intended to seat around one hundred and fifty people. Most of these would be in chairs either side of the central aisle, with additional space in the stage area and in the choir gallery.

The altar was to stand on a raised dais, the whole of which could be partitioned off by folding shutters running the full width of the hall to create a separate sanctuary. Here there was space for six seats on either side of the altar for use on weekdays.

There were to be two stained glass windows, both at the east end: the larger, high above the altar and the smaller one, lower down behind the tabernacle in a recessed apse. It is not specified in the 1982 plan what the windows were to depict. However, one drawing shows a figure (perhaps Christ or St Joseph) depicted in the lower window, and what appears to be the Sacred Heart in the larger window. Elsewhere, reference is made to the incorporation of a lily and a carpenter's square - symbols of the church's patron.

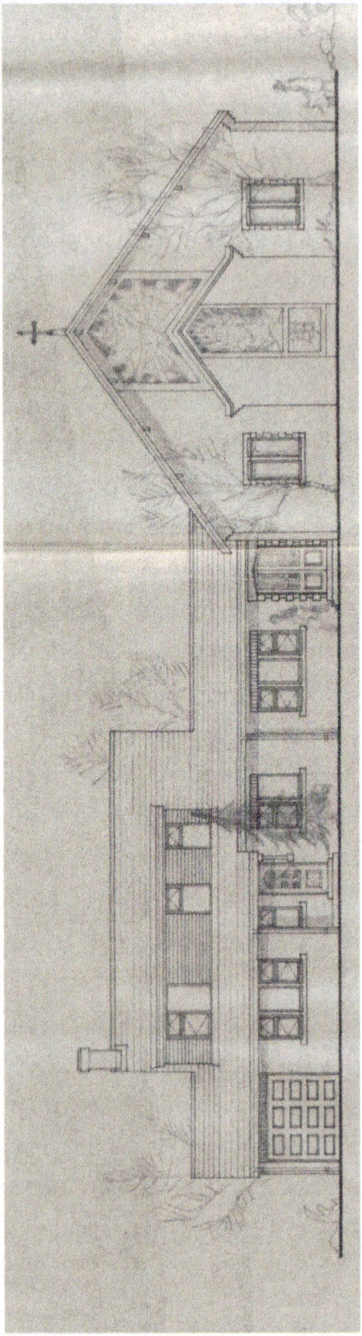

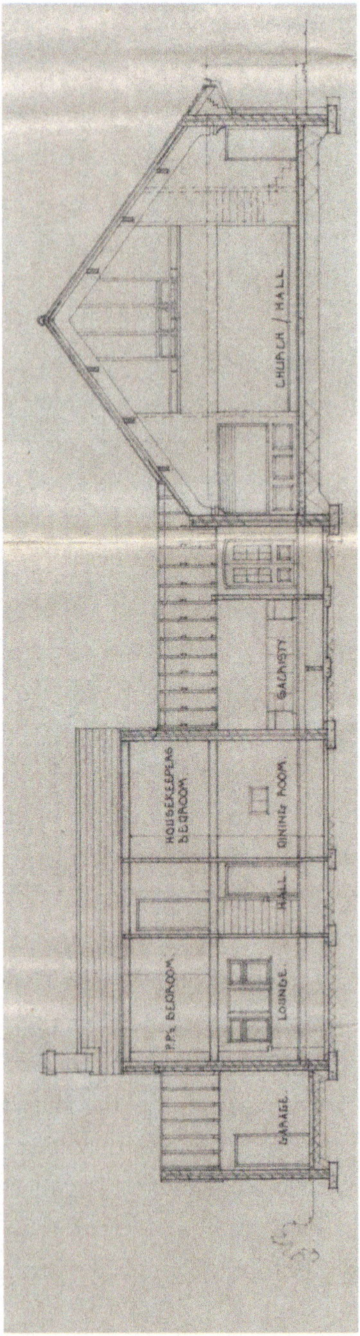

Above: Elmete Social Club before the construction of the access road.

Left: East elevation and corresponding section of the presbytery and church. The external view shows the intention to have two stained glass windows at the altar end of the church.

§ § §

A fundamental stumbling block for the entire project was reaching the site. The existing access was deemed unacceptable by the planning authority, and as the cinema building didn't reach all the way to Low Street, its demolition would not provide space for a new road without the roadside shops also being demolished.

The development of the Selby coalfield and the expected growth of the village meant that many new houses were the offing. One such development was on council owned land adjacent to the church site. With the local authority (now Selby District Council, which had replaced Tadcaster Rural District Council in the local government reorganisation of 1974) planning to build a road just to the north of the Elmete Social Club for the new housing development, a spur road could be added to access the church site.

However, this road was dependent on unlocking a 'ransom strip' of land. This was being held for a large sum in compensation by someone who the architect, Stephen Langtry-Langton, in an exasperated letter to Bishop Wheeler, referred to enigmatically as 'an entrepreneur (who shall remain nameless)'. It seems likely that the 'entrepreneur' in question was a Mr Shevill, secretary of the Sherburn club, as there followed a protracted series of correspondence between church, social club, local authority, architect, estate agent and diocese.

The deadlock was finally broken, in Langtry-Langton's words, by 'nothing short of a miracle', when Selby District Council issued a compulsory purchase order (CPO) to acquire all the land required for the road access and housing scheme to the north of the parish's site. The council agreed that the new church could make use of the new access road in return for the car park, planned for the cinema site, being made publicly accessible so that it could be used by shoppers during the week and churchgoers on Sundays.

It seemed like progress was finally being made. Yet, Father Foskew's transfer to St Joseph's in Barnoldswick in the summer of 1983 meant the unenviable task of tying up the multitude of loose ends and finally seeing the project over the line would fall to the parish's third priest since the project began.

§ § §

Father Paul Moxon was known as a 'Worker Priest'. Well-built with a head of thick, dark hair and aviator-style spectacles, he had the jovial plainness of speech that is often associated with those possessing his Yorkshire accent. He had spent four years in London training to be a teacher and achieved an external degree before he 'got the idea to train to be a priest'. After an interview with The Right Reverend George Patrick Dwyer, the then Bishop of Leeds, he was sent to the seminary of Saint Sulpice in Paris. Fortunately, he had studied French as part of his degree, which stood him in better stead than some of his less linguistically able compatriots.

Life in the seminary was hands-on from the word go. As more mature seminarians, Paul and his fellows were sent to nearby parishes and expected to help out in whatever way they could. This included the education of young people. One of the central principles of the French Republic is the separation of state and religion. For that reason, the country's education system is secular by law. However, it was permitted for Catholic pupils, who wished to receive religious education, to be taken out of school on a Thursday morning to participate in lessons provided by the parish. For the next four years, he applied his teaching experience in this new setting, all the while learning himself.

Upon return to the Diocese of Leeds in 1967, the newly ordained Father Moxon was appointed to the cathedral as a curate - a member of the clergy engaged to assist the parish priest. His time as curate is perhaps the shortest in the cathedral's history. Merely three hours after his appointment, Father Moxon was due to go on holiday and while he was away the Bishop decided that he should instead be sent to the parish of St Augustine's in Harehills. It soon became apparent that he and the parish priest there were not well suited, so to utilise his teaching degree, Father Moxon was transferred to St Bede's secondary school in Bradford.

At a loose end during the summer holidays, he was invited

to be second driver on a coach trip to give some of the city boys the opportunity to experience the Scottish countryside. These plans ultimately fell through but the bus licence he had acquired added another string to his bow. With the summer still ahead of him, he was encouraged to approach the Wallace Arnold coach tour company and began work as a seasonal driver.

It was around this time that Father Moxon became involved with the Bradford Churches' Industrial Mission - an ecumenical organisation aimed at providing ministry in places of work and preaching the Gospel in a manner relevant to people's everyday lives. As the mission was already being coordinated by an Anglican vicar and a Methodist minister, Father Moxon, as a Catholic priest (and one with a bus driver's licence), proved a welcome addition. With the Church in the era of Vatican II being called to look outwards, Father Moxon put the case to Bishop Wheeler and it was agreed that he could take on a role in the churches' Industrial Mission full time, funded by his summer work for Wallace Arnold.

While some no doubt raised their eyebrows at the idea of a coach-driving priest, Father Moxon received personal approval from the very top. During a particularly memorable trip, he drove a group of sick and disabled pilgrims to Rome onboard a 'jumbulance' (a specially converted ambulance coach). Parking in St Peter's Square, the pilgrims were blessed by a private audience with Pope Paul VI, who offered to pray for Father Moxon's ministry.

For ten years, he balanced his ecumenical mission work with employment on coach tours, occasionally puzzling holidaymakers who were left wondering whether their driver had a twin brother who was a man of the cloth. It was a demanding life and in time he began to wish for something more settled.

Meanwhile, Bishop Wheeler was keen that the drawn-out project in Sherburn-in-Elmet should be completed. As Father Foskew headed to his new parish, Father Moxon, by now in his early forties, was sent to finish the job. Remembered by parishioners as dynamic and never one to mince his words, he seemed ideal for the task. What he little realised, as he later wrote to the Bishop, was 'the vexed history of the project'. While 'not enamoured' of Langtry-Langton's work himself, he had to admit that the architect had 'put in a lot of effort on our account', which had not yet been paid.

The first few months of Father Moxon's life in the parish were not easy but he soon came to the conclusion that it would be 'disastrous to thwart the aspirations of the people in respect to a new church'. A building committee, comprising John Styles, Michael Clarkson and Tony Bolton (husband to Marian, who helped run the Saturday school), was established to try to drive the project forward.

Reading the letters written at this time, it is possible to feel the enormous sense of frustration, verging on despair, of those involved in the development. Towards the end of November 1983, Bernard Whalley drafted, though did not send, a letter to Bishop Wheeler on behalf of the parish council. In it, he voiced concern that planning permission was still being held up due to haggling over the number of parking spaces to be made available on church land and who should pay for them. He implored the Bishop to intervene, requesting that 'all the interested parties meet together at Selby [District Council] to formulate a solution' and conclude the planning stage as soon as possible.

To the parishioners it must have seemed that after a decade of exertion, they had got almost nowhere.

§ § §

As 1983 drew to a close, the council development adjacent to the church site was progressing well. The road was in and housing nearing completion. Yet, the church was still in limbo.

Through no small amount of negotiation, a meeting between Father Moxon, Monsignor Murphy, the diocesan estate agents, the various officers of the council and the District Valuer and Valuation Officer was agreed for early in the new year. On the 14th February 1984, Father Moxon was informed by Michael Buswell, of the diocesan estate agents, Oliver, Kitchen & Flynn, that planning consent had at last been obtained. Furthermore, the District Valuer was prepared to recommend that the Council grant the road as a right of way in return for the construction of the public car park.

Although this meant the access problem had at long last been solved, the final major hurdle was financial. The extensive discussions, planning applications and compulsory purchase orders had cost a considerable amount of time, and as the saying goes, time is money. It was starting to look as though even Father Foskew's more paired-back ambitions might be in doubt.

The funding for the project was to come from three sources. The first was the sale of the old presbytery, which it was hoped would cover around a third of the cost.

The second was the development of the Sherburn site. In addition to the church and adjoining presbytery, the planning consent included permission to build five shop units on the site of the soon to be demolished cinema. Like the church, these plans would evolve and take time coming to fruition. By 1985, a courtyard of seven shops with maisonettes above was being proposed. However, the present houses and flats of Corn Mill

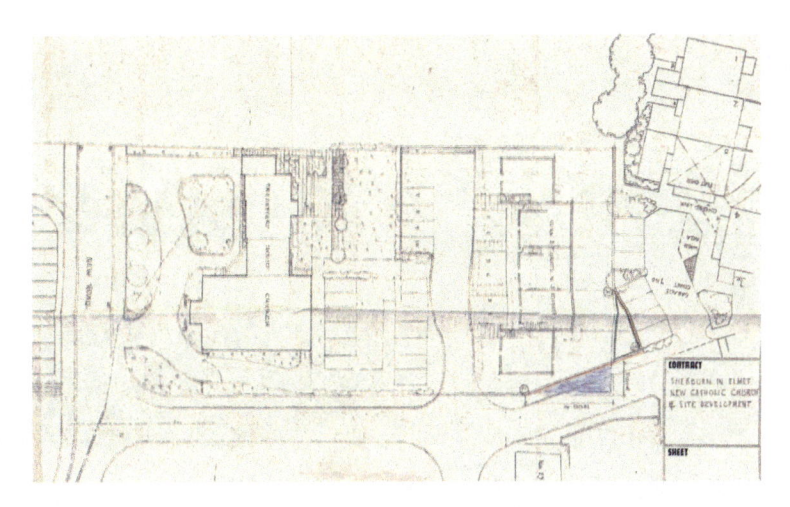

Above: Proposal for shops behind the church (November 1984). The shaded land would have been sold to extend Church Mews and provide access to additional flats beyond.

Below: Plan for shops with maisonettes on the former cinema site (February 1985). Neither of the plans were realised.

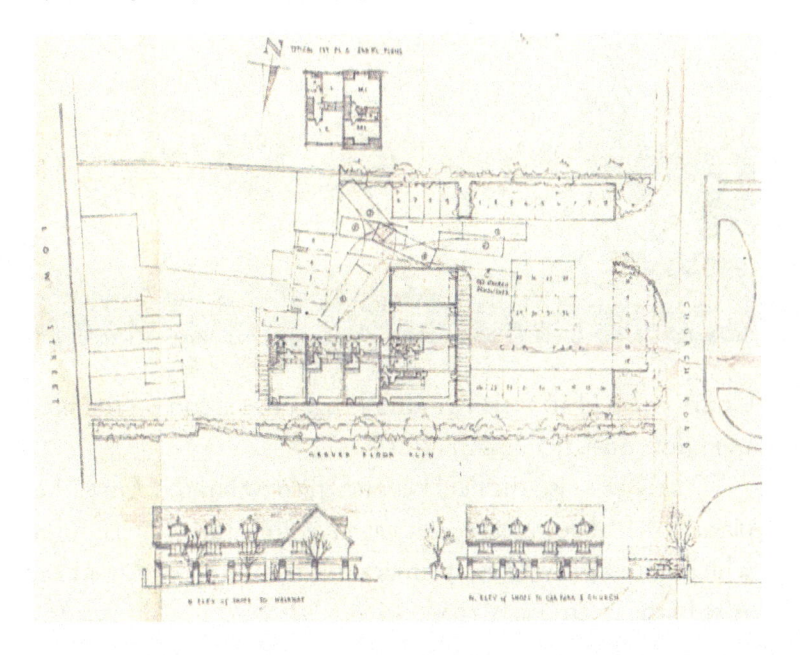

Above: The new car park after the demolition of the old cinema.

Below: The rubble of the Mill Shop, Low Street (1990). The church had been completed but the cinema site was still undeveloped.

Court - named after the windmill that once stood on the site - were not constructed until 2003.

There was also the field beyond the new church. On earlier plans, this had been marked out as a possible site for two houses, which could provide supplementary income should the need arise in the future.

The remaining money, however, would have to be raised by the parish. The community rallied to the cause. Rita Dawson's aunt, Anne Raines, was a parishioner at The Immaculate Conception, Scarthingwell, for over forty years. She often spoke fondly of the fundraising efforts, summing up the spirit of the time with the phrase 'everybody came together - it was wonderful'.

There was certainly no shortage of fundraising initiatives - fashion shows, whist drives, treasure hunts, jumble sales, tombolas and coffee mornings. There were fayres for all seasons. Derek and Maureen Clancey, who ran the local milk round, prepared dairy hampers to be raffled off. A 100 club lottery was organised, and the South Milford Country Club played host to a fundraising dinner and auction, with Bernard Qualter as auctioneer.

Perhaps the boldest suggestion came from longtime parishioner, June Denby. Always as well-dressed as she was well-spoken, June was a regular figure at Sunday Mass in Sherburn-in-Elmet until her death in 2021 at the age of 98. For many years, she was an organiser for the local branch of the Royal British Legion, having served as a staff driver in France in the months after D-Day, for which she was later awarded the Legion d'honneur.

At a parish meeting, June suggested there might be someone in the parish willing to do a sponsored parachute jump to raise money for the new church. All eyes fell on John Styles. As a former soldier in the Parachute Regiment, he seemed the obvious choice. Not a chance. He explained that in the army he had undertaken fifty jumps, all of which he had survived unharmed. He was not going to risk a fifty-first. The idea was dismissed.

Even with the best efforts of the parishioners, there was a need for additional funding. In a report to the diocesan Financial Commission - the body responsible for overseeing income, expenditure and investment across the Diocese of Leeds - Father Moxon set out the desperate need for a new church and the financial constraints placed on the parish. In addition to the bills involved in the day-to-day service of the local Catholic community and the upkeep of the primary school in Barkston Ash, the closure of St Camillus school meant the parish was also 'now fully responsible for Scarthingwell Church. Can we,' he asked, 'be responsible for a new church as well?'

. 4 .

Construction

When the builders laid the foundation of the temple of the Lord, the priests in their vestments were stationed to praise the Lord with trumpets. - Ezra 3:10

By the beginning of 1984, there was still no definitive way forward. On the last Sunday of February, the parish council of the Immaculate Conception was presented with a table of options for the future:

OPTION 1

Description: Do nothing. Stay exactly as we are - cinema at Sherburn; church at Scarthingwell; school at Barkston Ash; chapel at RAF Church Fenton; isolated presbytery.

Pastoral: Your priest is isolated from the main centre of population; limitations on worship and community activity in Sherburn due to unsuitable building.

Financial: Repairs to be done at the school and at Scarthingwell Church and presbytery.

Timescale: /

Comment: This option will not help us to be effective witnesses to Christ in Sherburn. We can sit on our assets of land and they will increase in value, but the risk is that there will be nobody to benefit from them. We need a 'suitable focus for our community, for those who come to Mass and for those who don't. Your priest needs to be among you in order to serve you.

***

OPTION 2

Description: Sell the presbytery and buy a suitable house in Sherburn for your priest, for daily Mass and meetings. Sell the whole Sherburn site and seek a suitably large place (village hall/other church) for Sunday Mass(es). We would have to rent this facility.

Pastoral: *Your priest would be among you. Scarthingwell church would be the site of our main liturgical celebrations and we could see to its maintenance. The Mass would be assured in Sherburn.*

Financial: *None. The cost of a house would be offset by the sale of the presbytery. Sale of the whole Sherburn site would put us into profit and assure the future.*

Timescale: *3-6 months*

Comment: *We would have no church building as such in Sherburn but we would have a focus for our people on the presbytery which would not simply be the priest's house. We would retain Scarthingwell church and bring it up to standard as we would have money for repairs there and also for the school at Barkston. We would be dependent on others for the venue for our Sunday Mass in Sherburn.*

***

OPTION 3

Description: *Approach the Methodists for a joint shared church/hall on our site. Buy a house for your priest nearby. Sell the presbytery at Barkston; keep Scarthingwell church as the main centre for worship.*

Pastoral: *Your priest would be among you. He would have to work more closely with other ministers and Christians. We would have to agree on times and usage of plant.*

Financial: *Half of project costs with legal provision on ownership.*

Timescale: *5 to 10 years?*

Comment: *This option is attractive. We could achieve more together by pooling resources. It would demand a lot closer relationship that we have at present and it is possible that there would be considerable opposition from both parties' members. Such arrangements do exist elsewhere in the country but are very difficult to establish where there are existing communities.*

***

Option 4

Description: *Sell presbytery at Barkston and our other releasable assets. Keep Scarthingwell church and Barkston school and go ahead with our project at Sherburn (i.e. presbytery and church/hall).*

Pastoral: *Your priest is among you and you have a focus for the Mass and other activities in an acceptable place.*

Financial: *We would have to accept a large debt in addition to paying our way on a day to day basis.*

Timescale: *Selby D.C. are prepared to reach an agreement with us and allow us access.*

Comment: *If we go for this option we must decide if we are to go ahead with the Langtry-Langton scheme, which has immediate approval. We could begin within 3 to 6 months at the latest. This scheme would be in the order of £230,000. A systems building by Stocks Bros. could be cheaper and we are looking at how much cheaper. But we would have to resubmit plans to S.D.C. so there could be delay.*

***

OPTION 5

Description: *Build a 2 to 3 class school on our Sherburn site (we would have to purchase some more land). Use the school for Mass on Sunday. Scarthingwell church would be retained, Barkston school closed and the site sold.*

Pastoral: *This gives a focus in Sherburn. A priest's house would be bought in Sherburn and he would be among you. More parents would be willing to send their children to our school.*

Financial: *15% of project.*

Timescale: *5 years +*

Comment: *This is an attractive proposal but it is difficult to assess how easily it could be effected given the present spending cuts, etc.*

***

OPTION 6

Description: *Develop Scarthingwell church and presbytery. Sell the Sherburn sit and approach the Anglicans for use of their church on Sunday in Sherburn. Encourage people to come to Scarthingwell from Sherburn (car or hired bus).*

Pastoral: *Sherburn stays isolated. Difficult to form a community.*

Financial: *We would be in profit.*

Timescale: *6-12 months*

Comment: *The sale of St. Camillus school at Scarthingwell and whoever the new owners are could be a factor in favour or against this option.*

***

It was decided to push ahead with the existing project but it was clear that further cost savings were essential.

On the 13th March, Father Moxon and the parish committee met with the architect Stephen Langtry-Langton. It came as a pleasurable surprise that Langtry-Langton could achieve a fixed tender price of £150,000 for the church and presbytery building, plus the professional fees the firm had incurred over the previous eleven years. The parish's realisable assets, including presbytery, the old cinema church site and two house plots were expected to come to £120,000. This left a shortfall of £30,000 - a difference that not even a sponsored parachute jump was likely to make up.

That weekend, Father Moxon wrote to Bishop Wheeler to update him on the situation and the fact that the parish was still 'some way short of being able to cover the whole costs of the project, which is now reduced to its minimum'.

The design certainly had been stripped back drastically. This was not only vital from a financial perspective. If the parish was to receive diocesan support, it was necessary that it be seen to be making cost savings too. Gone was the large stained glass window above the altar. The remaining, smaller one was to have a simple, abstract design, which when the sun shone from the east would nevertheless bathe the sanctuary in coloured light.

The folding shutters across the front of the altar were abandoned. Instead, two tall concertina doors divided the apse from the altar. The altar itself was designed to be dismantled so it could be stored behind these doors when the hall was being used for secular activities.

The number of doors had also been cut back to a more moderate amount. The confessional wall in the sacristy was erased. The second female toilet had been done away with. Even some of the walls inside the church were to remain unplastered - a minimal decorative effect being achieved by having every fourth row of bare bricks standing slightly proud of the rest of the wall. Phase two of the development - the hall at the rear - was shelved altogether.

Tony Bolton, part of the group trying to identify savings, later recalled that one of the few cost cutting suggestions not to be accepted was a reduction in the size of the priest's bedroom. The original three bedroom layout had already been reduced to two, so when asked whether a priest needed a double bedroom at all, Father Moxon simply smiled and quipped,

'I haven't given up hope on the Pope yet'.

In any event, the dormer design was such that the financial savings of changing from double to single bedrooms would have been negligible.

The future of the church now lay in the hands of the Finance Commission and whether they would be willing to free up the necessary capital for building work to begin.

On 28th March, with a decision still pending, Stephen Langtry-Langton took the unconventional step of writing to Bishop Wheeler directly. He did not mince his words. While he spared the Bishop the 'almost interminable list of the machinations of dealings with land owners, crooks and various Planning Authorities' that has been necessary to get the project to this point, he implored him to 'prevail on the Finance Commission to allow us a bridging loan, which would facilitate implementation of the work and aspirations of us all over the last decade'.

Left: Design for the simplified stained glass window and dismantlable altar.

Right: The stained glass window from the outside with the larger plain glass window above.

The Bishop's answer came two days later. His letter was brief but it was the answer that everyone in Sherburn has long been waiting for. Bishop Wheeler reassured the architect that he was entirely behind the project: 'This is to say go ahead because it is a pastoral necessity and the good Lord will provide.'

§ § §

The weather was overcast in the early evening of Monday 19th March 1984 as the parishioners of Sherburn-in-Elmet gathered to celebrate the feast of their church's patron, St Joseph. After Mass, the congregation processed from the chapel and, singing hymns, made their way over the field behind the old cinema. The position of the new church had already been staked out in the grass with string marking the line of the foundations.

One of those present was Rosalie Treble. She had been shown the site some time previous by Emma Clarke, a 'lovely, very humble' elderly lady, who used to look after the cinema church. Like other parishioners, she knew the many years of tribulation surrounding the church's development and also felt the sense that it may never be built. As she showed Rosalie the field, she gave voice to both the fears and faith of many.

'This is where our church will be one day. Not in my lifetime, but in yours.'

Margaret Holt's son, David, as altar server, carried a turf cutter in one hand and holy water in the other. Once the hymn had finished, Father Moxon blessed the site. Then, taking the spade, he turned to the seventy-nine year old Mrs Clarke.

'Will you do the honours.'

She dug the first sod. Despite her earlier scepticism, she did live to see the church finished and died the following year. The builders, Clayton Bowmore Ltd., moved onto the site and the construction process that so many parishioners feared may never start, finally got underway.

Above: Cutting the first sod. Father Moxon blesses the site before construction of the new church begins.

Left: Father Moxon with altar server David Holt. His mother, Margaret, can be seen wearing a floral cardigan in the background (and looking into the camera in the photograph above).

§ § §

Now that the building work had started, the estate agents, who had originally been instructed back in January 1982, were finally given the green light to commence the sale of the presbytery. Despite the dilapidated state of some parts of the building, three offers were received from prospective buyers who saw the potential. By early June, an offer from a Mr and Mrs Dennis had been accepted. Contracts were exchanged with a delayed completion date to allow time for the construction of the new presbytery in Sherburn.

Yet, things were not to run entirely smoothly. The day after Father Moxon received confirmation of the contract exchange, the diocesan estate agent, Michael Buswell, received a letter from Tony Lawton of Grays solicitors. He explained, 'somewhere along the line I think there may have been a misunderstanding'. The completion date that had originally been suggested was the 1st November, at which point Father Moxon would have to vacate the presbytery. However, the date on the contract to which the purchasers agreed had been brought forward to 1st October.

Quite how such a misunderstanding had occurred is unclear but the contract had been signed. In a letter explaining the matter to Father Moxon, Buswell tried to put a positive spin on the situation, suggesting it might be 'advantageous to you to have the proceeds of the sale at an early date to meet your other commitments'. While this may have been true, it raised the question of where Father Moxon was now supposed to live between the leaving the old presbytery and the completion of the new one.

He found the answer in Scarthingwell Church. Jutting out from behind the main entrance is a single-storey extension. It is simply built with concrete lintels and unadorned rectangular window panes, but the stone walls, probably reused from elsewhere on the site, and slate roof means it does not look terribly out of place. This extension was originally built as a chapel for the Poor Clare Sisters in 1948, as evidenced by the two candle mounts built into the wall on either side of the alcove in which the altar would have stood. Later, it was used as a wood workshop when St Camillus school occupied the site of the old hall and after that as a storeroom for the church.

Measuring only five metres by ten, it was hardly a luxurious living space. Nevertheless, there was room enough for Father Moxon to store his possessions and bed down for six weeks. The lack of kitchen facilities was a challenge but the toilet in the church sufficed for sanitary purposes. To him, it was all a bit of an adventure, 'rather like camping out'.

Above: The parish room of Scarthingwell Church in which Father Moxon spent six weeks 'camping out'.

While Father Moxon settled into his temporary abode, building work on the new church continued apace. A framework of steel girders was erected first and then the walls built around it. As parish priest, he kept an eye on developments, periodically visiting the site.

As the walls rose, scaffolding was assembled and, on one such visit, Father Moxon was invited up to admire the progress. By this point, the bricklayers had reached about bedroom height. As he neared the top of the ladder and prepared to step out onto the scaffolding, he made the mistake of putting his hand out to steady himself. The only recently mortared bricks shifted and, to the alarm of the builders and Father Moxon alike, he pulled down a portion of the wall.

Unfortunate though this was, it was nothing compared to the disaster that had befallen the church in Garforth, now sister-parish to St Joseph's, some years before.

Above: The steel frame of the church is assembled before the brick walls are built.

The Church of St Benedict was completed in 1964 and all was set for the official opening. School children had been in to rehearse the afternoon before the first Mass and altar servers reported hearing creaking noises. That night, a design defect combined with the weight of heavy snow caused the roof to collapse. Mercifully, the church was unoccupied so no one was injured, something for which parish priest, Father Alban Rimmer, understandably offered prayers of thanks. It would take another three years for St Benedict's to be rebuilt. Despite not going down well with the builders, Father Moxon's mishap in Sherburn was rectified rather quicker and as Advent approached so too did the building's completion.

The final structure differed slightly from the earlier plans but the adjoining presbytery and church concept is maintained. Built of pale red brick, with white wood and uPVC window frames and a long, sloping, red concrete pantile roof, the exterior stands out little from the surrounding houses. On the outside of the church's east end, below the stained glass window, is set a recessed foundation. Now obscured by plants, this stone is carved with a cross, the horizontal arms of which are longer than the vertical ones. The red painted door to the presbytery matches the double door to the church. The dormer, with cream painted render and exposed black timbers, nods to a mock-Tudor style.

The layout of the presbytery has a trait described by Father Moxon as 'classic Langtry-Langton: doors everywhere' - though fewer than there might have been. Upon walking through the front entrance one is met by four more doors. Doubling back on oneself to the left is the downstairs toilet. Next, moving clockwise, is the door to the living room, which opens into the middle of the room directly opposite a brick fireplace on the far wall. The ceilings are comparatively low - not enough to be uncomfortable but still low enough that a taller visitor might feel slightly claustrophobic.

The stairs to the upper floor are opposite the main entrance, alongside the door to the kitchen, which has access to the garden at the rear. The final door, on the right as one enters, leads to the dining room. For many years this was used as a parish room for children's liturgy, confessions and housed the altar of repose - used after the Mass of the Lord's Supper on Holy Thursday. This room connects to the sacristy and on to the church.

The upper floor is also unusual. At the top of the stairs the landing turns back towards the front of the building. The guest bedroom is on the left and the main bathroom straight ahead. To the right is the parish priest's bedroom - a double room with a couple of steps down through an open doorway into an office space below the eaves.

The church itself is a large hall. The parquet floor of African hardwood was apparently salvaged from another church. The kitchen by the entrance is simpler than in earlier designs and is

Left: Church of St Joseph the Worker shortly after completion in 1984.

Right: The lectern created by Tony Mattison (photo taken in 2024). The carpet on the altar dias was originally green.

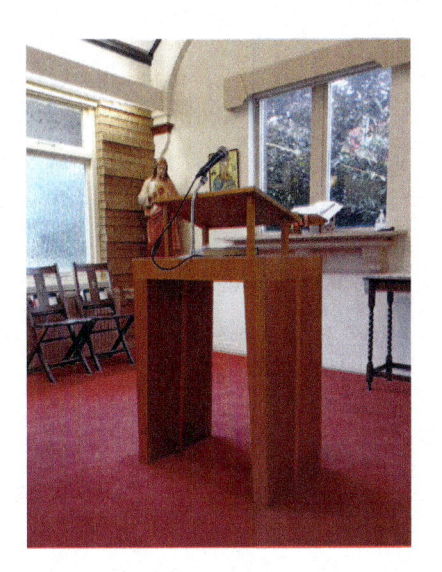

accessed by a standard door rather than a folding counter top. The folding shutters of the serving hatch face out under the gallery rather than towards the altar.

The carpeted dias, on which the altar stands, can be partitioned from the sanctuary, when being used as a stage - perhaps the most obvious physical indication of the church's intended multi-purpose design. The lectern, to the left of the altar (as viewed by the congregation) was created by local carpenter, Tony Mattison, who in his later years would delight the children of the parish by appearing as Father Christmas at Christmas fayres.

The side windows of textured Minster glass, providing light but maintaining privacy, are separated by unplastered brick buttresses. These correspond to the trusses of the steel frame. The internal boxing around the upper part of the frame is painted black to stand out from the white of the rest of the ceiling. The five-light, triangular headed, clear-glass window at the front of the church is reflected in the design of the three-light window at the west end, which lights the choir gallery.

From a solely architectural perspective, the Church of St Joseph the Worker, Sherburn-in-Elmet, may be of limited interest. However, the religious and social value it represents to the community that built it can not easily be overstated.

§ § §

On the afternoon before the opening, the church was a hive of activity. Although the building work had been completed, there was still much to be done in preparation for Mass the following day. Construction dust needed to be swept up and floors mopped. Chairs had to be set out, and the large number of cardboard boxes and other packages needed to be disposed of. It was not only practising parishioners who lent a hand. For example, Rosalie Treble's husband, Geoff, despite not being a Catholic, was roped in to clean the windows and put up the curtains in the presbytery.

Inside the main window above the altar a crucifix had been erected. In fact, two such crucifixes of different sizes had been ordered as Father Moxon had been unsure which size to use until he had seen them *in situ*. With one in place, the other was put away so that it could be returned to the supplier.

Father Moxon, who had been called out for the afternoon, returned to a group of rather sheepish looking parishioners. They very apologetically explained that in the confusion of clearing the church the spare cross, packed back into its box, had ended up on the bonfire of cardboard rubbish. In the circumstances, Father Moxon was sure the Almighty would be forgiving. For the Catholic parishioners of Sherburn-in-Elmet, the long years of waiting were finally over.

.5.

Renewed and Built Up

I was glad when they said to me, "Let us go to the house of the Lord!" - Psalm 122:1

The opening of the new Church of St Joseph the Worker was a joyous occasion. Early on the morning of Saturday 22nd December 1984, Tony Bolton drove over to Lawnswood, Leeds, to collect Bishop Wheeler, who was to concelebrate Mass with Father Moxon. This was to be a blessing rather than a consecration - a reflection of both the fact that the building was intended to double as a hall, and that the parish remained dedicated to the Immaculate Conception.

Above: After the opening Mass. From left: Reverend David Post, Anglican Vicar of Sherburn; Bishop William Gordon Wheeler; Mrs Emma Clarke; Mrs Molly Catterall; Father Moxon; Monsignor John Murphy. Front: David and Stephen Whalley.

Right: Booklet created to commemorate the new church.

They arrived to a packed church. The opening hymn, 'Come Holy Ghost', was led by Bernard Whalley playing the guitar, as he would do almost every Sunday for the next three decades. His and Janet's sons, David and Stephen, were on the altar serving their first Mass. It was not only regular parishioners who were present. The construction of the village's first Catholic church, seemed, in Father Moxon's words at the time, 'to have made people aware of our existence and encouraged them to come and worship'. In keeping with Father Moxon's previous ecumenical mission, Reverend David Post, the Anglican Vicar of All Saints church, was also invited.

Fr Paul Moxon outside Sherburn's first purpose-built Catholic church — the Church of St Joseph the Worker. (T5661/1.

Priest settles into new church

SHERBURN'S church history entered a new era on December 22 with the opening ceremony of its new Catholic church. And by the end of this month its Priest, Father Paul Moxon should be well and truly settled.

When Father Moxon came to the area 13 months ago from his post as industrial chaplain in Bradford, he was faced with the task of overseeing the building and transfer to a new church in the village.

This had to take priority over any other ventures he had but now, at last, he can see the results of his efforts with congregations of one hundred plus and rising.

"The congregation love the new building, but after what they have worshipped in in the past, it is hardly surprising. The erection of the village's first, very own Catholic church also seems to have made more people aware of our existence and encouraged them to come and worship," said Father Moxon.

Above: Local newspaper article celebrating the new church.

To commemorate the opening, a booklet was produced. In it, Father Moxon wrote of a new era. The Catholic parishioners of Sherburn-in Elmet were delighted to have a fitting place of worship 'as an expression of our faith'. Nevertheless, he wrote, the building - bricks and mortar - was not an end in itself. With this new beginning it was the people of the parish, 'as God's people, who had to be renewed and built up'.

The cover of the booklet was illustrated with a plough, to symbolise Scarthingwell and the farms of the parish, and a pit wheel, representing the growth of Sherburn and the development of the Selby coalfield. This was, however, the time of the 1984/5 miners' strike. Although the area was not affected anywhere near as severely as other parts of the country, the impact was still felt. A food-bank trolley stood outside the shops across from the church on Low Street and life was hard for individual parishioners employed in the coal industry. It is notable that of the two pictures used to decorate the front of the commemorative booklet, it is the plough that has endured.

§ § §

The new church became the heart of an active Catholic community in Sherburn. The fundraising efforts continued, not just to cover the debts on the new church but also to pay for much needed repairs to the Immaculate Conception in Scarthingwell. Having not long since celebrated its 130th anniversary, the church was suffering from rising damp, rain damage over the sanctuary, and £800 was needed for repairs to the organ alone. The restoration and redecoration of the church would finally be completed in March 1990.

A leaf through the event accounts gives an indication of the wide range of activities organised by the parish at that time.

Between 1984 and the end of 1988, there were summer and Christmas fayres, garden parties, race nights, coffee and wine evenings, frequent raffles, a Halloween disco, a pottery party, a clothes and linen party, a musical night, and, in what must have been one of the best dressed parishes of the diocese, no fewer than three fashion shows in the space of a year.

Weekly engagements were also part of an active parish social calendar. These included a music group, led by Bernard Whalley, Sunday evening bingo, and a Thursday night youth group. The latter had evolved from the Saturday school and was initially run by Pauline Roe and Susan Ferguson, both

Right: Poster advertising the 1987 Summer Fayre.

Below: Raffle ticket listing the prizes available in the 1985 'Grand Autumn Draw'.

of whom had sons who attended. The younger members of the parish took part in Youth Masses at St Anne's Cathedral in Leeds; retreats to the Skipton youth centre; and day trips, which included a range of outdoor activities such as sailing, dry-slope skiing and climbing.

The local Vincent de Paul Society arranged visits to elderly parishioners to help them out with tasks, such as shopping, and provide company. The driving force behind this was Dennis Harker, a veteran of D-Day, who arrived in Normandy only six hours after the first landings. He also fulfilled the role of sacristan - opening the church and making the necessary preparations for Mass.

Father Moxon continued the practice of house Masses, which, as the name suggests, were occasions when parishioners would welcome others into their home for the celebration of weekday liturgy. These had been started by his predecessor, Father Foskew, but harked back to the country house tradition of worship from a time when the public profession of the Catholic faith was still illegal. Newer practices, such as Lenten talks and joint carol services, were encouraged to foster Christian unity and good relations were built up with the other churches in the village.

Although he had no live-in housekeeper, Father Moxon was greatly assisted in domestic matters by Helen Harvey (known to her friends as Ilene). For Father Moxon, his friendship with the Harvey family was about more than just help with cooking and cleaning. Their household was a place where he could get away, at least for a short time, from the burden of his duties, and even forty years on, they still keep in touch.

Ilene and her husband, Tony, had moved from Scotland. Before settling in the parish, he had been a footballer and made a handful of appearances for Dundee F.C. between 1965 and

1966. The two of them would later establish Rainbow Nursery just outside Barkston Ash, however Ilene's main employment at this time was as cook at the primary school. One morning, Father Moxon received an anxious telephone call from Ilene, who explained that the company that prepared the meals had delivered sausages for the children's dinner. It was a Friday.

The Church in England and Wales had moved away from the centuries-old practice of abstaining from meat on Fridays in 1984 (the fast would be reintroduced in 2011), but Catholics were still obliged to undertake an alternative act of penance in its place to remember Christ's Passion.

To throw the sausages away would be a terrible waste and the children would still need something to eat. Father Moxon considered the conundrum.

'Give the sausages to the kids. There'll be very little meat in them anyway.'

§ § §

A very literal high point for Father Moxon came as a result of the parish's association with RAF Church Fenton. During the Second World War, the airfield was one of the network of fighter bases tasked with defending the industrial areas of South Yorkshire and the Humber estuary. In addition to being home to the first 'Eagle squadron' of American volunteers, the first all-Canadian and all-Polish squadrons were based at Church Fenton.

Being less than three miles from the church at Scarthingwell, care of the pastoral and spiritual needs of Catholic personnel fell to the local parish priest, who acted as chaplain - a responsibility that continued until the station chapel closed at the end of March 1992.

A Roman Catholic Mass was offered every Saturday evening in the multi-denominational chapel, which was dedicated to the seventh century Saint Paulinus, first bishop of York, and situated between the gym and amenities centre. As Father Moxon wrote in his Christmas message of 1989, 'God, as it were, sandwiched between the physical and the practical'.

By the late 1980s, RAF Church Fenton's primary role was as a flying school training would-be air force pilots in two-seater Jet Provosts. One of the instructors, Dick Norris, remembered by colleagues as a 'thoroughly decent bloke with a great sense of humour', was a regular at the Saturday evening Masses offered at the airbase. He had not long since handed in his notice to the RAF in order to become a commercial pilot when he remarked to Father Moxon,

'We haven't flown you, have we, Father?'

'What do you mean 'flown me'?' replied the priest.

The instructor explained that in order to maintain their skill level, instructors were required to undertake a couple of flights themselves every month. He had one such flight coming up and there would be a spare seat available.

So it was that the following Monday, having received a briefing on how to use an ejector seat and a height check to ensure that he was not so tall that he would leave his knees behind in the cockpit should his newly acquired knowledge have to be put into action, Father Moxon found himself on Church Fenton runway seated in an RAF jet. On his lap, as instructed, was his camera.

At 10:30 am, a couple of miles down the road, the pupils of Barkston Ash Roman Catholic primary school gathered in the playground to watch their parish priest fly overhead. Alex Dadge (née Bolton) was one of the children in the playground that day. She remembers waiting with excitement on what was for her one of many memorable days at the school. The aeroplane appeared over the horizon and within a few seconds was gone, roaring off in the direction of the Lancashire border.

Above: Pupils of Barkston Ash Catholic Primary school, including Alex Bolton in the front row.

Beneath Father Moxon, rushed the patchwork fields of the parish, then the suburban sprawl of north Leeds, and the rugged hillsides of the Yorkshire Dales. Approaching the village of Bentham, they descended to circle the Church of St Boniface where his friend, Father Kennedy, was standing and waving outside the presbytery. Then, back east until they swept over the giant, golf ball-like radar domes of RAF Fylingdales on the North York Moors, to conduct some low-level flying exercises and various aerobatic manoeuvres. These completed, they headed for home. As they neared York, Dick turned to his passenger to inform him that strictly speaking it was forbidden to fly over York Minster, but as he was leaving the RAF he would bend the rules on this occasion. The jet roared towards the city walls and Father Moxon took out his camera.

Father Moxon's flight was not the only instance of RAF involvement in the life of the parish. With a large number of young children in the congregation, Christmas fayres and parties were an annual feature. Central to the planning of any such occasion was the question of where to find a costume for Father Christmas. The organising committee was informed that RAF Church Fenton owned just such a costume, which the church was free to use.

However, shortly after the offer was made, a minor hiccough was discovered. Church Fenton's costume had been lent to RAF Scampton, just north of Lincoln, some sixty miles away by road. Fortunately, Dick Norris and Ian Scott, another regular at the Church Fenton Mass, had an idea. In the absence of the traditional reindeer, they would send a jet.

A route was planned and booked in as a training flight. A Jet Provost was dispatched, landing at RAF Scampton long enough to collect the costume before making the return trip, ensuring that Father Christmas was able to put in an appearance, much to the delight of the children.

Left: Same outfit – different event. RAF Church Fenton's Father Christmas costume, on this occasion worn by Flying Officer Dave Christie with Mrs May Voice on his knee at a Senior Citizens' Christmas Party.

94

§ § §

On Sunday 1st July 1990, Father Moxon announced to the congregation that he was to leave. The Bishop - the Right Reverend David Every Konstant, who had succeeded Bishop Wheeler five years earlier - had appointed him to the parish of St Joseph in Wetherby commencing at the beginning of September. He had served the parish for seven years and in his parting message expressed his gratitude for the generous love, warmth and support he had experienced in that time.

His successor was Father Gerald Creasey. At fifty-six, Father Creasey was a few years Father Moxon's senior. He had worked for many years as a teacher at St Thomas Aquinas School in Leeds before becoming parish priest at Cleckheaton and Morley, gaining what his predecessor described as 'a wealth of experience and pastoral zeal'.

To introduce himself to the parish, he chose the words of Cardinal John Henry Newman: 'In this world, to live is to change, and to be perfect is to change often'. This, he explained, referred not only to changes from place to place, but also to the changes that occur while growing in faith 'as we journey along the pilgrim way of life'.

Father Creasey appears to have felt his way had been smoothed by the warm welcome he received. Nevertheless, it was not lost on him that when a parish priest is called to pastures new - 'even if only a few miles up the A1' - that a certain sadness is understandable, but also that 'one of the wonderful consolations of our Faith is that we are never completely separated'.

§ § §

Above: Painting of the Church of St Joseph the Worker gifted to Father Moxon on his departure from the parish.

In writing this history, I thought long about the degree to which I should include my own recollections, if at all. After all, this is not my story but that of the entire parish. On the other hand, it would be impossible to act the part of a truly objective historian when describing people, places and events that have featured so heavily in my own life.

I was born into the parish towards the end of 1991 and was baptised by Father Creasey the following February. I remained a parishioner, and for many years an altar server, until heading to university eighteen years later.

Indeed, one of my earliest memories took place in the Church of St Joseph the Worker. I must have been only about two or three years old. My mum, Amanda, had stood up during Mass and walked to the lectern to deliver a reading. Whatever feeling of abandonment I felt in my toddler mind, I determined that I should join her. I set off in pursuit as fast as my little legs could carry me, only to be scooped up by Henry Spence in a move that would have done the England rugby team proud and returned to the care of my dad, Adrian.

§ § §

For the two years Father Creasey served the parish, life continued much as it had done. Perhaps the change most notable at the time was the closure of the RAF chapel in Church Fenton. This meant that Mass was no longer being said in the parish on a Saturday evening and so a 6pm Mass was introduced in Sherburn on a trial basis.

Another significant, though less widely reported, change was the rededication of the parish from the Immaculate Conception to St Joseph the Worker. With the new church and presbytery, it was perhaps natural that St Joseph's had become the main focal point of the parish. Sherburn was growing and Father Creasey was keen to promote the church as the cornerstone of the Catholic community in the village. As a result, he agreed with Bishop Konstant that the parish should be renamed after the new church.

This seems to have been a fairly organic shift to reflect the changing realities of the parish, rather than a grand affair. Indeed, the only subtle indication in the bulletins occurs in October 1990 when the order in which the two churches were listed was reversed.

On top of his duties as parish priest, Father Creasey was also responsible for the care of his elderly mother, who lived in Leeds. The frequent travelling back and forth was a considerable strain, especially as his mother's health deteriorated. In early October 1992, he announced quite suddenly that to ease his anxieties the Bishop had transferred him to St Patrick's in Leeds as part of a three priest team covering two parishes and St James's Hospital. In his stead, Father Michael Lynch arrived - his first appointment as a parish priest. However, he too left within two years.

Above: The wedding of Katie Adams and James Grantham at St Joseph the Worker (17th July 1993).

Father David Massey's appointment lasted a little longer. He came late to the priesthood and his route was an unusual one. Born in Cairo in 1936, where his father was serving in the RAF, the young David was educated in England at Gilling Castle, North Yorkshire, and Ampleforth College. Here he was a distinguished athlete. He returned to Africa during his National Service when he was commissioned in the Devonshire Regiment. After leaving the army, he served in the police in South West Africa (now Namibia) and later pursued a career in commerce working for, amongst others, a company that made light fittings, until he felt drawn to the religious life.

He returned to Ampleforth pursuing his vocation at the Abbey but realised that his true calling lay as a parish priest. He was ordained in July 1990 and served at St Anthony's and St Augustine's in Leeds before being appointed to St Joseph the Worker in 1994.

He was a private and often unassuming priest, but despite his quiet nature, parishioners remember him with respect and affection. While parish priest in Sherburn, Father Massey also undertook work for the Diocesan Finance Office and Clergy Health Scheme, but by 1997 the first signs of serious illness had appeared and he was briefly moved to St Aelred's Church, Harrogate, before having to take sick leave. At his funeral Mass, Bishop Konstant reflected that despite his long illness, Father Massey remained cheerful and at peace until his death at St Gemma's Hospice in 2003 on the Feast of Our Lady's Nativity.

. 6 .

The Poet Priest

By wisdom a house is built, and by understanding it is established; - Proverbs 24:3

Jeanne Goodall had not been to St Joseph's before. The week before she moved from Wakefield, she decided to go to Mass in order to get a feel for the parish. So it was that one Sunday towards the end of Lent in 2015, she found herself walking through the red painted wooden gates and up the tarmac drive of the church. Inside the ivy covered porch, she was met by an elderly looking man with a head of thinning white hair.

'Hello,' he said, 'who are you?'

Jeanne introduced herself.

'Are you new to the parish or just visiting?'

She explained that she was about to move to the area. His eyes smiled at her through wire-framed glasses.

'Well, you're very welcome. I'm Father Michael, the parish priest.'

Jeanne was taken aback. With his ordinary clothes and open collar, he did not seem like any priest she had encountered. While he would don Liturgical vestments for Mass, Father McCarthy was rarely seen wearing a dog collar.

At communion, he leant towards Jeanne and whispered.

'What is your name?'

She told him. As Mass drew to a close and Father McCarthy prepared to say the final blessing, he rose and looking towards Jeanne said,

'...and I'd like to welcome Theresa, who is new to the parish and I'm sure we'll all make her feel very welcome.'

Despite the mix up, ~~Theresa~~ Jeanne laughs as she recollects her first experience of the church and remembers with immense fondness the warmth with which she was received by priest and parishioners alike.

After Mass, while teas and coffees were served in powder-blue cups and saucers from the kitchen counter, Jeanne was approached by Joan and Michael Dobson.

'Hello Theresa.'

'I have to tell you,' she replied, 'it's not Theresa, it's Jeanne. He got it wrong.'

'Oh, I shouldn't worry too much about that.'

Jeanne is by no means alone in having happy memories of her arrival and of Father McCarthy. In fact, this depth of affection is widely shared by many parishioners.

On moving to the parish in 2000, Fran Bostyn thought the parish priest seemed familiar. She asked if he was the same Michael McCarthy who had been chaplain at her secondary school - St Joseph's College in Bradford - some twenty years prior. He smiled and replied,

'The one and only Michael McCarthy.'

Having known him for a further eighteen years, Fran agrees that he was certainly one of a kind.

§ § §

Above: Family photo of Father Michael McCarthy.

On Not Being a Singer

I've always wanted to be a singer,
To let my voice follow the song as far as it could,
Glide out over the crowd. I can do it all right in my head.
Last night in the mirror inside the sacristy door I was
Ray Charles. 'I can't stop loving you'. It was perfect.
Except for the voice, and the fact that I wasn't black.

Willie Nelson. Maybe I could do that, or Pavarotti,
The way he belted it out before the World Cup.
But not like the old tramp on O'Connell Street that night
Before the All Ireland: his arms outstretched, head thrown back,
His slurred eyes oblivious to the crowds as they stream past,
And no sound whatsoever coming out of his mouth.

My father was a fine singer. His father before him
Taught all his children to sing. As a boy he had wanted to
Go off and sing like Caruso, as John Mc Cormack did later on.
He stayed on the farm, and raised thoroughbred horses instead.
My uncles and aunts could all sing. My father's songs were
'Hard times come again no more' and 'The ship never returned'.

At the Races - Michael McCarthy
Smith/Doorstop Books, (2009)

§ § §

Right: Michael McCarthy as a young priest.

Below: Some of the many First Holy Communions celebrated at St Joseph the Worker during Father McCarthy's time.

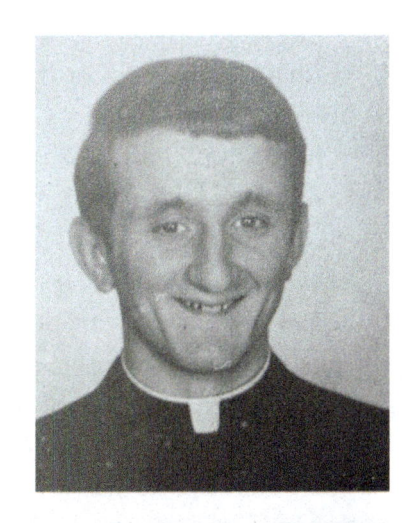

Father Michael McCarthy's childhood was spent on the family farm in rural County Cork in the southwest of Ireland. His uncle, with whom he shared his name and his birthday, was a missionary. The young Michael listened to stories of his travels in China and resolved that he too would be a priest.

After finishing school, he left Cork to study at St Patrick's College, Carlow. In his memoir, he recalled that the training when he arrived was more or less the same as it had been for the last four centuries, and described ethos as 'inward looking, lest our vocation be contaminated by the world'.

However, like Father Moxon, Father McCarthy trained in the era of the Second Vatican Council. The influence of new Catholic theologians was beginning to be felt on the seminary curriculum. The sense that they were on 'the cusp of great changes in society and in the church', excited Michael and his fellows. The College was changing and by 1969, his final year at seminary, there was much more contact with the outside world and the older seminarians were being given greater responsibility.

The more conservative, traditionalist outlook he had sometimes encountered as a child was giving way to a less austere, more compassionate one. The legacy of these years remained imprinted on his theology. In his own words: 'God is not a distant figure or a judge, but a lover who has loved me from the beginning. Jesus of Nazareth, as well as being the Son of God, is my brother. I too am a beloved son of God.'

The affirming ethos of the seminary suited him and in that well-rounded, supportive community his confidence grew. In addition to his studies, he joined the drama society and later wrote 'it is my belief that I learned to be myself while pretending to be someone else'.

As a young priest he wrestled with anxiety and self doubt.

Yet, at the same time this understanding of human frailties, coupled with the time he put into carefully crafting each homily, made him an excellent communicator.

He was alive to the challenges of faith. That sometimes it can be a struggle to believe, and that when someone is faced with such doubts the answer is not condemnation but love and reassurance. In his homilies on the Sundays after Easter, Father McCarthy would often speak with great compassion about Saint Thomas, who despite his disbelief was addressed by Jesus 'not with reprimand but with mercy'.

He articulated the subtleties of belief, explaining the way in which faith and doubt are inextricably intertwined. They are not opposites but 'the inside out of one another'.

Blessed are those who have not seen and yet believe. Thomas did not believe, yet he confessed his doubts and allowed them to surface. Doubts which, when they are 'avoided, unacknowledged... weigh heavily on us'. In Father McCarthy's eyes, Thomas did not display the certain arrogance of someone over sure in his belief or disbelief, as the case may be. Instead, he was an 'honest agnostic', whose personal act of faith led him to exclaim 'My Lord and my God'. In so doing, he was 'much closer to humility and therefore much closer to true faith'.

§ § §

The death of his ten-year old brother, James, in an accident when Michael was just four had a profound and long-lasting effect on him. Any description that might be given here of his journey of healing would be pitifully inadequate compared to his own eloquent testimony in his memoir, *Like a Tree Cut Back*. Nevertheless, it was on this journey that he began to write poetry.

During an eight-year stint as spiritual director at Ushaw College, he started going to poetry readings in Newcastle and Durham. In the company of others, he honed his craft. In June 1995, with his time at Ushaw coming to an end, Father McCarthy had his first poem accepted for publication.

Keen to develop his poet self, he wrote to Bishop Konstant asking to take a sabbatical. He spent the following year in Edmonton, Canada, and upon his return read about The Patrick Kavanagh Award - a competition for poets who had not yet published a full manuscript. Having loved Kavanagh's poems all his life, he put together a pamphlet under the title *Birds' Nests and Other Poems*. To his surprise and immeasurable delight, he won. In 2003, these poems became his first published collection.

Ann and Peter Sansom co-directors of The Poetry Business - a writer development agency and independent publisher - first met Father McCarthy in the late 1990s when he started attending Poetry Business Writing Days at Byram Arcade in Huddersfield. He continued to attend these workshops regularly and became a valued member of their Writing School, an eighteen-month advanced poetry course for published writers.

Ann and Peter were proud to later become his publishers, under their Smith|Doorstop imprint. They brought out four collections of Father McCarthy's poetry - the pamphlet *Cold Hill Pond*, which later formed part of *At the Races*; *The Healing Station* written during his three-month residency with patients with dementia and strokes, and their carers at Adelaide and Meath Hospital in Dublin; and *The Bright Room*, published shortly after his death in 2018.

It was not just his poetry that Ann and Peter admired. With his characteristic mix of warmth and empathy, wisdom and quick humour, he offered advice and support for their business and to them personally.

When their eldest son, David, died suddenly in his sleep, Father McCarthy was away on retreat. He told them that he had gone back to his room and decided, against his own rule, to check his emails. When he saw that Peter had written to him only minutes before, he felt that he needed to go see them as soon as possible. He sat with the family and supported David's siblings, Katherine, Tom and Mary (who he always called 'Your Ladyship'). He advised Ann and Peter throughout the funeral arrangements and conducted a beautiful service. Their love and admiration is evident, so too is their gratitude for his practical kindness and wisdom at that terrible time.

Over time Father McCarthy became a good friend to the couple and one of their happiest times was when he rang to say that he had just fallen off his chair in surprise while reading the Saturday Guardian. Hilary Mantel had chosen his latest collection as a Book of the Year:

Michael McCarthy's poems in The Healing Station *(Smith/Doorstop) move through the blighted linguistic landscape of the stroke and dementia sufferer, patiently restoring sense and wholeness. Oddly cheering, like flowers in winter.*

Hilary Mantel, Best Books of 2015
The Guardian (Saturday 28 November 2015)

Along with Father McCarthy's niece, Ita Mac Carthy, and Richard Scholar, Ann and Peter were entrusted to be his literary executors. Between them they oversaw the posthumous publication of Father McCarthy's 'remarkable prose memoir'.

§ § §

Theologically Speaking
i.m. Tess Carr 1921 - 2003

The Church: there beside the lake
hunchbacked against the wind
since eighteen-fifty-four.

In the background
Cardinal Wiseman's cedar
growing taller every year.

Close by: the grass cut
the undergrowth cleared away
the small wooden cross now obvious.

'Who's buried here?' I ask.
'Bernadette', she says.
My eyebrows puzzle.
'The cat.'

Realising this wasn't your average cat
I hesitate. 'It's not a matter
of being small-minded or anything
but theologically speaking
Jesus didn't die for cats.
Could the grave be marked say by a shrub?'

Over a medium-sized pause
my suggestion is dismissed.

'She did enough for this Church.
Everybody loved that cat.'

Theology would have to please itself.
May Bernadette have eternal rest.

At the Races - Michael McCarthy
Smith/Doorstop Books, (2009)

§ § §

In October 2004, the parish marked the one-hundred and fiftieth anniversary of the consecration of the Church of the Immaculate Conception and St John of Beverley, Scarthingwell. While the opening Mass lasted two and a half hours, the jubilee celebrations spanned two and a half days. These began with a Friday Mass with the children of Barkston Ash primary school. The former first floor teacher's residence had recently been converted to classrooms and, after Mass, Father McCarthy blessed the new facilities.

The following day, Bishop Arthur Roche presided over the official anniversary Mass, during which sixteen young parishioners received the Sacrament of Confirmation. The church, as it had been one-hundred and fifty years prior, was packed. Father McCarthy drew attention to the tree planted by Cardinal Wiseman which, perhaps emblematic of the parish, had grown to a magnificent height and continued to flourish. In his homily, the Bishop quoted Saint Paul's letter to Timothy, reminding those who were confirmed to 'fan into a flame the gift that God gave you' and invited them to return with their

Above and right: Timeline created by Janet Whalley and pupils of Barkston Ash school to celebrate the Millenium depicting both parish churches.

Below: Parish picnic in the garden of St Joseph's (2017).

children and grandchildren in 2054 to pass on the rich heritage that they had received.

Throughout my own time at Barkston, the two churches played a central role in the spiritual and social life of the school. Scarthingwell, being the nearest, was where Mass was celebrated on special occasions. Out of the school gates, we would make our way down the grass footpath that started parallel to the playground, emerging onto Church Street down a couple of steps in the shadow of one of the ancient stone barns of Croft Farm. Then, in single-file down the narrow pavement past the gates of Barkston Towers before winding our way through Scarthingwell Park to the church.

This journey was also utilised by the children in Key Stage 2 (juniors) for sponsored walks to raise money for the school. Being in Key Stage 1 (infants) in the summer of 1999, my class remained in school. However, my mum, Amanda, offered to help out as one of the adult volunteers on the sponsored walk. The route took them through the village to the church, where they would stop for a break, before heading back to school.

It was during a kickabout outside the church that mum struck the notorious shot. Had the goalkeeper been six foot two he surely would have made an excellent save. Unfortunately, he was closer to four foot six and the ball sailed over his head and straight through the parish room window.

It has been said that nothing travels faster than the speed of light with the possible exception of bad news. This was certainly true in this instance. I have no idea how in the absence of mobile phones I managed to hear the news before she had got back, but as my class walked out of the school hall, I saw the older children returning from the sponsored walk. I strode up to my mum and demanded to know with all the admonition that a seven year old could muster,

'What did you do?!'

The incident led to my sister and I banning mum from playing football within a hundred yards of a window for several years after, but it did wonders for my own street cred.

Later that evening, mum phoned Father McCarthy to apologise and to offer to pay for the damage. He was immensely relieved. He had been fretting that one of the children might have spent the evening being reprimanded by their parents for something that had certainly been an accident.

This innate ability to understand the world through the eyes of a child, also came through in Father McCarthy's writing. Around the same time that his first collected volume, *Birds' Nests and Other Poems*, was published, he also wrote two stories for children. These were poetic retellings of *The Story of Noah and the Ark* and *The Story of Daniel in the Lions' Den*, both beautifully illustrated by Italian artist Giuliano Ferri. He brought the early drafts into school and read them to the children asking for feedback. He listened to our comments, treating us as peers and valued literary critics.

The Church of St Joseph the Worker also retained close ties to the school. Not only was it where many of us made our First Holy Communion, but the dual purpose of the building meant it was the setting for many non-liturgical events too. End-of-year concerts, school discos and, of course, nativity plays, some of which were truer to scripture than others. Jethro Standley, a former pupil at Barkston Ash, vividly remembers the pinnacle of his theatrical career coming in Year 5 as one of a trio of Elvis Presley angels, complete with perfectly quaffed rubber wigs.

§ § §

Nativity At Barkston Ash

Credit St Francis of Assisi
who started the whole thing off
with an Ox and a Donkey
borrowed from his friend Giovanni
at a cave near Greccio in twelve twenty three.

In this year's Nativity Play
the teller of the tale is a Robin,
who has got the news from a Dove,
and includes all the usual characters,
Shepherds and Sheep, Camels and Kings,

along with a flock of birds
of indeterminate identity,
and a cluster of stars
calling themselves The Milky Way.
The birds take their radar by the stars.

As they get near to Bethlehem, and see
the gifts of Gold, Frankincense and Myrrh,
they realise they should have brought a gift.
The three kings remind them they are birds.
They bring the gift of song.

And so they proceed to the stable
and there among the assembled cast
offer their gift to the baby boy,
an up tempo number called
We Found Jesus.

Prize for the most original costume
goes to Joe, a Seabird, his
floppy yellow webbed feet
made from his mother's
rubber gloves.

The Bright Room - Michael McCarthy
Smith/Doorstop Books, (2018)

§ § §

Above: One of the many Nativity plays performed by children of Barkston Ash school and 'Barkston Sings the Victorian Music Hall'.

Chris Power was headteacher at Barkston Ash between September 2013 and April 2021. Each year, the school celebrated Education Sunday with a special Mass at St Joseph's. Children would attend in school uniform and lead the readings, prayers and offertory procession. The school choir led the musical aspect of the worship, and Father McCarthy often invited Chris to speak during the Homily about Catholic education, school life and nurturing the spirituality of the children at Barkston Ash. He remembers these as always wonderful occasions with the church filled with the families of children and parishioners.

The first such school Mass during his headship was in February 2014. Afterwards, he received an email from Father McCarthy:

'Outstanding sounds a bit trite for what took place at St Joseph's this morning. It was much more profound than that. It was wonderful to hear everyone singing together and the choir gave a memorable performance which was appreciated by us all.'

Chris' own reaction, published on the 'latest news' section of the school website, shares Father McCarthy's sense of delight:

'It was a real joy to see the church packed with children and their families... Following communion, part of the school choir performed a song to the congregation called 'Our God.' It was truly moving. The whole Mass was beautiful and enriched, and was a real embodiment of school and parish working together.'

He recalls other special moments, including the Christmas productions that took place at St Joseph's each year. The Reception and Key Stage 1 children retold the Nativity, while Key Stage 2 pupils made Advent Presentations. It was an ideal setting in which to tell the Christmas story through drama and song.

Above: Pupils and parishioners celebrate a school Mass at St Joseph's. Chris Power is on the right playing the guitar.

Left: Chris Power recieving a farewell book from parishioners on his departure from Barkston.

Below: Barkston Ash school discos held in the church / hall (early 2000s).

During this period, Sacramental preparation for First Holy Communion was completed in the church on Tuesday evenings. Andrew and Liz Lowe were the Catechists, who prepared the children. Meanwhile, Chris joined the parents for religious input from Father McCarthy. For an hour and a quarter, they enjoyed spiritual nourishment from 'a wonderful storyteller'. These sessions were never something that a headteacher had to attend, but for Chris it was 'always a privilege to listen to the wise reflections of Father McCarthy'.

§ § §

In April 2018, Father McCarthy was diagnosed with pancreatic cancer. He had successfully undergone surgery for colon cancer twenty-three years earlier but this time it was incurable. In a letter written to Father Conn Ó Maoldhomhnaigh - President of his alma mater, Carlow College - he described that in his final weeks he was blessed with 'a calm spirit and a deep gratitude for the life I have been given' as well as 'a burst of creative energy'.

It is perhaps thanks to this energy, creative clarity and his skill as a writer that he was able to complete his final book on Friday 8th July 2018 - three days before he died. *Like a Tree Cut Back* is a deeply moving work, weaving together biography, history, poetry and spiritual meditation. As his niece, Ita, put it, 'an extraordinary testament to an ordinary life well lived'.

§ § §

Last Will and T.

And to you my high horse, I leave
this original saddle, the stirrups thrown in
for luck, as well as the rest of the tack.
And after you have galloped off, I leave
the echo of your hooves to the heather
and what's left of the morning air
to the ducks in the water-lilied lake.

And I leave the ring of my doorbell
to the empty room, to the stained carpet
where Charley knocked over the soup
when he got drunk on emptiness
until he was full of light. To the rest
I leave the benefit of the doubt.
Now and at the hour of my death.

At the Races - Michael McCarthy
Smith/Doorstop Books, (2009)

. 7 .

Not an End, but a Beginning

Like living stones, let yourselves be built into a spiritual house. – 1 Peter 2:5

Father Steven Billington arrived to a parish in mourning. He was appointed Parochial Administrator - a priest who takes the place of the pastor when a parish becomes vacant - in Autumn 2018 following the death of Father McCarthy.

Change is difficult in a time of grief. The arrival of a new priest with his own way of doing things has the potential to cause ripples at the best of times. For parishioners and priest, navigating such a delicate atmosphere was not always easy.

There were also a number of managerial matters that had fallen by the wayside during his predecessor's illness and were now in need of attention. Father McCarthy, for all his qualities, was not a natural born administrator and accounting was never a strong suit. Even as a child, he liked history more than he liked sums, and the keeping of parish records was often a job for tomorrow.

This was an daunting task and, while some parishioners will admit that it took time to adjust to their new priest, they also recognise Father Billington's significant efforts in ensuring that the parish administration and finances were on an even keel for the years ahead.

On a personal level, my family owes him a particular debt of gratitude. Like me, my sister Lizzie, went to primary school in Barkston and always dreamed of getting married at Scarthingwell, where she had also made her confirmation.

When her partner, Rich, proposed, they were living outside the diocese. Unfortunately, realising her dream proved far less straightforward than they had hoped. My sister was distraught and, with a heavy heart, she and her fiancé began to explore the possibility of a wedding elsewhere. Meanwhile, our mum reached out to Father Billington. He replied to her that same evening.

'Leave it with me.'

With the same quiet effectiveness with which he approached the parish accounts, Father Billington overcame the various hurdles, made all the necessary arrangements and delivered a beautiful wedding service.

Right: Father Billington waits at the door of Scarthingwell church.

Below: The wedding of Elizabeth Whitwood and Richard Say at Immaculate Conception (13th April 2019).

His appointment as Parochial Administrator was only ever temporary and as September 2019 approached, he made plans to leave for Rome.

Father David Bulmer, a kind but also rather shy and quiet man, was chosen as his successor. He moved into the presbytery in Sherburn shortly after Father Billington's departure, though ill-health meant he was delayed taking up his pastoral duties. In the meantime, the parishioners made-do as best they could.

Since Father McCarthy's time, there had been a growing question mark over the future of the parish. A shortage of priests meant that a number of other parishes in the diocese had been merged or were being jointly administered. Without the guarantee of a long-term successor, lay parishioners began to feel a greater burden of responsibility for ensuring a viable future.

In the years since the church had opened, the broad range of parish activities had dwindled. Christmas fayres still took place most years - raising money for church upkeep, such as re-carpeting the altar dias and purchasing new curtains, as well as donating to the Sherburn visiting scheme, which delivered meals and provided activities for elderly members of the community. Nevertheless, the non-liturgical calendar was far quieter than it had once been.

One initiative to reinvigorate parish life was the creation of a CAFOD Live Simply group. Fran Bostyn took a leading role in its inception and describes the aim as to 'build the parish community' through social events, like parish walks, picnics, and meals out. There was also a focus on care for the environment and the wider community. Collections for the local food bank were introduced and lift sharing to Mass was encouraged.

However, these efforts would soon come to an abrupt halt.

Top: Parish walk, Scarthingwell (May 2019).

Right: Ecumenical Walk of Witness (Good Friday 2019).

Below: Meal out at The Oddfellows Arms – the last parish event before lockdown (January 2020)

§ § §

Lent 2020 was a time of great global challenge. On Sunday 8 March 2020, the Vatican announced the suspension of all public Masses in Rome, in line with the measures taken by the Italian government, to tackle the COVID-19 pandemic. Holy Week celebrations were cancelled. The following day, Pope Francis began the daily live-streaming of Mass from his residence, setting an example for other affected countries to follow. As the crisis worsened, churches across the globe took similar action as the world fought to contain the spread of the disease. The Apostolic Penitentiary relaxed the requirements to receive the Eucharist and Confession for people affected by lockdowns.

At the height of the outbreak in Italy, the Pope imparted an extraordinary *Urbi et Orbi* blessing, usually reserved for the joyous occasions of Christmas and Easter. In images appropriate to the solemnity of the times, the world watched as His Holiness walked alone through the steadily falling rain in a deserted St Peter's Square to the platform from which he prayed for the health of the world.

For a short time, normal life stopped. Towns and cities fell almost silent. Social gatherings were curtailed. Travel prohibited. Friends and families were prevented from seeing one another.

Jeanne Goodall thinks of the pandemic as 'a dividing line' in her time at St Joseph's. She had taken early retirement shortly after moving to the parish, which had given her the opportunity to get involved in various aspects of church life. Like most people, she remembers the pandemic as 'a very difficult time'.

Even after the church was reopened, first for private prayer and later for the celebration of Mass, things were far from normal. Everyone sat individually with seats set out two metres apart. Face masks had to be worn. Liturgical practices were adapted. The shaking of hands as the Sign of Peace was replaced by waving or a simple smile. During the Eucharist, consumption of the Blessed Sacrament was initially limited to the priest and when communion was reintroduced for the laity, it was strongly encouraged that the Host should be received into the hands instead of the normative way, on the tongue. It would take significantly longer before it was once again deemed safe for the congregation to drink from the communal cup.

Left: Paschal candle beside the altar at St Joseph's. Prayers were offered for the health of the world and an end to the pandemic.

Below: Smiles and fond memories at the socially-distanced launch of Father McCarthy's posthumous memoir, *Like a Tree Cut Back* (October 2021).

Administrative tasks were affected too. Prior to the lockdowns, it had been customary for those who counted money received at the collection to work in pairs. Jeanne was part of one of the three counting teams, paired with Pat Halliday. Every third Monday, they would meet in the sacristy of St Joseph's to count the donations offered during the Masses in Sherburn and Scarthingwell the day before. However, with strict social distancing in place that financial safeguard had to come second to reducing the risk of infection. Collection counting would instead alternate between counters, who were entrusted to work individually.

All social activities were cancelled. Many parishioners, particularly those who were elderly or who had health conditions, were understandably hesitant to return to public gatherings, and the parish struggled along with much reduced congregations.

Father Bulmer's health was also in decline and his retirement in mid-2022 led to the appointment of another Parochial Administrator. At the time of his arrival, Father Timothy Swinglehurst was also the Episcopal Vicar for Education, who on behalf of the Bishop provides episcopal oversight of Catholic schools in the Diocese of Leeds. His abiding memories of his brief time at the parish reflect the determination of the congregation to rebuild after the pandemic. Not only was he struck by how 'splendidly' he was welcomed, but also by the fact that, 'though a small community, so many people looked after and supported the parish that it was able to flourish with a priest only present on Sundays'.

While only another temporary appointment, Father Swinglehurst oversaw a post-COVID return to normality and steadied the ship long enough for a decision about the long-term future of the parish to be made.

§ § §

It's a weekday evening in April 2024 and I am sitting in a round backed armchair in the study of St Benedict's Presbytery, Garforth. Father Henry Longbottom enters and sets two mugs of tea down on the low, circular coffee table in front of me. Yorkshire Gold - a gift from a parishioner.

'Would you like a biscuit?' he says and disappears, returning a few moments later with a half-eaten selection box. I take a chocolate orange ring.

He is in his forties - about the same age Father Moxon was when he came to the parish. His hair, shaven to a fade on the back and sides, is black. So too is his nearly trimmed beard. The white of a dog collar pokes out at the top of his shirt, and I wonder to myself whether his black hoodie and dark jeans combo could be the twenty-first century's answer to the traditional soutane.

Over the next hour, we talk about philosophy, theology and our own backgrounds. He speaks with the zest and energy of a man who has found his calling and relishes it. At some point, he mentions that the fortieth anniversary of St Joseph's Church is approaching and we agree it would be nice to do something to commemorate the occasion. Perhaps a short book on the history of the parish?

The next time I meet Father Longbottom, he hands me a large, blue, plastic box containing the parish archives. It is filled to the brim with foolscap folders, account books and ring binders.

'Good luck.' he says.

§ § §

Above: Father Henry Longbottom at his ordination with the Right Reverend Marcus Stock, Bishop of Leeds, in St Anne's Cathedral.

Father Henry Longbottom was born in Huddersfield. His journey of faith began with a personal encounter with Jesus through reading the Gospels after being given a Gideon New Testament in a school assembly. Although baptised an Anglican, in his twenties he was drawn increasingly to Catholicism and at the age of thirty was received into the Catholic Church.

As a young man, Henry studied at St Peter's College, Oxford, before going on to practise corporate law for a firm in London. During this time his sense of vocation grew. At the age of thirty, he was Baptised into the Catholic Church and left his career in the legal profession to join the Jesuit order. He spent two years in novitiate in Birmingham, three years in London and a further two in Belgium but discerned that his true calling was to be a parish priest.

Father Longbottom was ordained in July 2020 - the first Catholic ordination in the country since the onset of COVID. His hopes of a huge celebration with hundreds of people had to be drastically slimmed down. Notwithstanding the need for social distancing, the ordination Mass in Leeds cathedral was a joyful occasion, not least because it was one of the first times people were once again able to meet in a space other than online.

After two short assignments to parishes in Leeds, Father Longbottom received a call from Bishop Marcus Stock appointing him to St Benedict's, Garforth, and St Joseph the Worker, Sherburn-in-Elmet.

This was not a merger of the two parishes, as had occurred in other parts of the diocese. The parishes of St Benedict's and St Joseph's remain distinct but are jointly served and administered by one priest.

As if to underline this fact, in September 2023, Father Longbottom was installed as priest to each of the parishes in two separate inductions: one at St Benedict's Church in Garforth and the other at the Immaculate Conception in Scarthingwell. A third welcome event - a bring-and-share supper - was held at St Joseph the Worker a little over a month later to allow parishioners to get to know their new priest in a less formal setting.

Father Longbottom's vision is that, as time passes, the communities he serves will grow in cooperation and mutual support, while retaining the distinctive character of the three churches. The concept of three distinct parts working together as one is hardly unfamiliar in Catholicism, and even in the year since his arrival, Father Longbottom has noticed a growing crossover between the churches as parishioners embrace the flexibility to come to Masses at different times. Occasional joint activities, such as an altar-server laser-tag trip, are also helping forge new links.

§ § §

Above: Social event at St Joseph's to welcome Father Longbottom.

Below: Statue of St Joseph the Worker on the upstairs gallery - the location for the next major building project.

After forty years the Church of St Joseph the Worker is starting to show signs of wear and the Immaculate Conception is once again in need of repair. With Father Longbottom jointly administering the parishes from Garforth, the presbytery in Sherburn is no longer required and parishioners offered a significant amount of free time and expertise getting it ready to be let out. The door between the sacristy and dining room has been blocked off, severing the internal link between house and church, and both rooms have been replastered and carpeted. The built-in cupboards that once lined two walls of the sacristy have been removed, greatly opening up the space for parish meetings, including Children's Liturgy on the first and third Sundays of each month, and confirmation classes.

Probably the most striking change to the church in recent years is the replacement of the stackable brown plastic seats with bench pews. These were donated from the chapel of the Little Sisters of the Poor in Headingley, which was forced to close following the discovery of reinforced autoclaved aerated concrete (RAAC) in their Mount St Joseph's care home and the building being condemned for demolition. Whilst this means the space at St Joseph the Worker is less flexible than when first designed, a number of parishioners have remarked that the change of seating adds a religious solemnity to the church.

The next major building project for the church is the reconfiguring of the upstairs gallery. While we share more tea and biscuits, Father Longbottom outlines the ambition for a glass screen to be erected to create a separate narthex, which can be used as a function space as well as a quiet area for parents with young children during Mass.

Scarthingwell too requires perennial upkeep, both structurally and in terms of day-to-day care. When Father Longbottom arrived, the parish room, where Father Moxon had

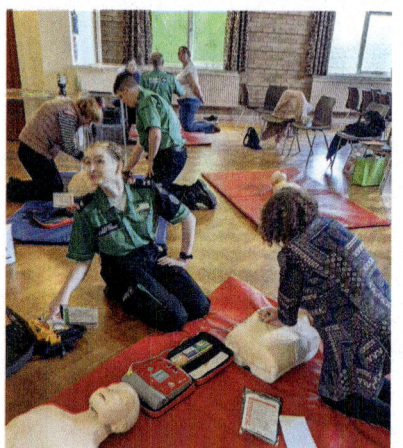

Above: Childrens' liturgy.

Left: Selby St John Ambulance Cadets teach parishioners lifesaving first aid skills (May 2023).

Below: Coffee morning at The Little Teapot in The Old Girls' School, Kirkgate (December 2022)

previously 'camped out', was stacked high with accumulated clutter. With the assistance of parishioners, this was gradually cleared and Terry O'Hearne has taken on the task constructing bookshelves and managing the room as a library.

As Father Longbottom speaks, it is clear that despite the need for a lot of work on the physical structure of both churches, he sees a lot of potential for the parish. Indeed, he says as much. The two different churches - St Joseph the Worker and the Immaculate Conception - are in his view a real asset to have in one parish, offering different but complementary experiences of worship. To Father Longbottom, they are as 'two lungs of the same body'.

Above left: Ecumenical Lenten Talks (March 2023).

Above right: Wedding of Karen Ambler and Paul Keay at St Joseph the Worker (September 2024)

The link between Barkston Ash Catholic Primary School and the Immaculate Conception remains strong. Children walk to Scarthingwell where Father Longbottom celebrates school masses every Wednesday.

The deep spirituality and acoustics of the Victorian church lends itself to the choral Mass. The Immaculate Conception was the setting for the Rudgate Singers' first Mass back in June 1996. The ad-hoc group, founded by Mike Forbester, focuses on restoring sacred music to its original liturgical context, and since December 2023 have sung Masses at Scarthingwell on several occasions.

Meanwhile, Sherburn-in-Elmet continues to grow. The village was redesignated as a town in 2022, and the establishment of an outreach group to make contact with Sherburn's newer population, as well as supporting a younger generation to take a lead in reinvigorating the church community is a core part of Father Longbottom's mission.

The last few years have been a challenge for the parish. The pandemic hit everyone very hard. Yet, one common theme amongst parishioners is a great appetite for renewal. Everyone with whom I have spoken over the course of writing this book has expressed a pride in the history and character of the parish. This character is not lost on Father Longbottom either:

'There's a deep spirituality. People really pray - it's not just a social grouping. Their faith has been nurtured.'

What is also evident is a desire for the community to grow, numerically and spiritually, for the future. The challenge lies in being able to, in Father Longbottom's words, 'empower people to be confident to carry out ministries themselves'. This is not only a practical requirement for the long-term sustainability of the parish. It goes to the heart of the renewed enthusiasm and strengthened sense of personal responsibility set out for the laity during the Second Vatican Council.

There is a sense in which, in the forty years since the Church of St Joseph the Worker was built, the parish has come full circle. After a difficult period, the years ahead are an opportunity to breathe new life into the parish. While Father Longbottom is in some ways a very different character from his predecessor Father Moxon, they share - albeit divided by a span of four decades - a drive and dynamism to build-up the parish and empower the congregation so they themselves may be 'a means to evangelisation of ourselves and our community'.

. Postscript .

In Reflection

For surely I know the plans I have for you, says the Lord, plans for your welfare and not for harm, to give you a future with hope. - Jeremiah 29:11

A few years ago, I visited Liverpool's Anglican Cathedral. It is an incredible building. Yet, standing in the nave with the pillars of pink sandstone towering above you, the altar seems as distant as heaven itself. The scale is awe inspiring but it is not built on a human scale. In such a vast and cavernous space, God can feel a long way away.

Similarly, some European cathedrals are adorned with a sensory overload of gold and marble to serve as a reminder of the glory of God, yet one must wonder if such grandeur might sometimes drown out the personal in the same way that it is nigh on impossible to meaningfully get to know a bride and groom on their wedding day. They are dressed in their finery and there is too much else going on. To build a relationship takes a humbler, quieter place.

There is an element in human psychology which states that a significant amount of what we think of as rational thought is in fact reverse engineering reasons to fit conclusions we have already reached based on instinct. Perhaps this is what I am doing.

However, the landscape I grew up in - the Vale of York with its flattish fields bounded by the rolling hills of Yorkshire's Wolds, Moors and Dales - does not seem to me to be one formed by a God whose message is one of might and subjugation. Maybe if I had grown up in a place dwarfed by nature - in shadows at the foot of a mountain, or on plains and prairies where the sky is almost all and the thin strip of land stretches uninterrupted to infinity - I might see things differently.

But nature's care and attention to detail - the shape of every flower, the changing colour of every leaf, the lilt of each bird's song - alongside the regard for the bigger picture seems to evoke the creativity and consideration of a craftsman. A carpenter.

The Church of St Joseph the Worker may at first glance seem an ill-fitting tribute to such a craftsman. The design is not particularly original and the decor is hardly ornate. Yet, the very lack of decoration also tells a story. Each unplastered brick and every pane of unstained glass is testimony to the dedication of the people of the parish coming together to realise a shared vision.

Above: Inside the Church of St Joseph the Worker – a space that 'lends itself to devotion'.

On a clear day, the large windows bathe the church in sunlight. It is a simple but elegant structure that, in Father Longbottom's words, 'lends itself to devotion'. It is human in scale and has a friendly, community feel that puts people at ease, whether they are life-long parishioners, visitors to the parish, or the growing number of non-Catholics who come to the church week in, week out.

This book originated essentially as a timeline of the construction of St Joseph's. However, the more people I spoke to, the more it became apparent that to focus on the building alone would be to miss out on the many human stories. Indeed, it would be to miss the point entirely. Without the congregation who worship within it, even the grandest of churches is reduced to little more than bricks and mortar. As Father Moxon wrote when commemorating the opening, 'the church is not an end in itself'.

Nor is a congregation an empty vessel. The priest may be a shepherd but his parishioners are far more than mere sheep.

Instead, a parish is a tapestry of relationships. Sometimes these may be imperfect, yet at best, these relationships are a communion of love and devotion.

Ultimately, this is not a story that one might find in a romanticised 'Lives of the Saints', in which individuals live an other-worldly existence of sinless piety. Instead, the history of the Parish of St Joseph the Worker, its two churches and congregations is a deeply human story of people acting with care, compassion and the occasional touch of eccentricity. It is a story of hope that serves as a reminder of what can be achieved in unity, and of the compassion we receive at our most human, flawed and faltering, to continue, even as we stumble, towards the divine.

Prayers to St. Joseph for Workers

Joseph, by the work of your hands
and the sweat of your brow,
you supported Jesus and Mary,
and had the Son of God as your fellow worker.

Teach me to work as you did,
with patience and perseverance, for God and
for those whom God has given me to support.
Teach me to see in my fellow workers
the Christ who desires to be in them,
that I may always be charitable and forbearing
towards all.

Grant me to look upon work
with the eyes of faith,
so that I shall recognize in it
my share in God's own creative activity
and in Christ's work of our redemption,
and so take pride in it.

When it is pleasant and productive,
remind me to give thanks to God for it.
And when it is burdensome,
teach me to offer it to God,
in reparation for my sins
and the sins of the world.

(Chosen by Father Henry Longbottom from the booklet 'Devotions to Saint Joseph' by Brian Moore, S.J., printed and published by the Society of St. Paul.)

Acknowledgements

This book would not have been possible without the involvement of a great many people, including past and present parishioners, and members of the wider community. I would like to thank Father Henry Longbottom for supporting this project, granting access to the parish archives, offering constructive feedback throughout the writing process, and being willing to share his aspirations for the parish.

I am especially grateful to everyone who was willing to be interviewed and whose recollections helped to bring this history of the parish to life: Father Paul Moxon, Margaret Addyman, Tony and Marian Bolton, and Jeanne Goodall.

Thanks to Warwick and Caroline Comer Stone of the Sherburn Photographic Archive, and Kevin Sibson of the Sherburn-in-Elmet Local History Society the use of so many historical photographs.

Reproduction of Father Michael McCarthy's poems is by kind permission of Ita Mac Carthy and The Poetry Business - a note of particular thanks to Peter and Ann Sansom, and Jessica Rollitt.

I am indebted to Peter Conway and John Styles, whose timelines of parish history were an invaluable starting point and to Robert Finnigan - Diocesan Archivist, Diocese of Leeds - for filling in further details.

Additional architectural information is drawn from *Taking Stock*, a project of the Catholic Bishops' Conference of England

and Wales to provide an architectural and historical assessment of churches in regular use for public worship.

I am immensely grateful to my parents, Amanda and Adrian, for a lifetime of love and support, as well as acting as proofreaders for this book.

Finally, I would like to thank everyone else who shared their memories, dug through family albums to find photos, or has helped in any other way:

Bibs Adams	Marie Marsh
Fran Bostyn	Emily Mattison
Alex Dadge	Kate Murray
Rita Dawson	Greg Page-Turner
Christine Dennis	Chris Power
Joan Dobson	Helen Rook
Michael Dobson	Lizzie Say
Maureen Elsworth	Rich Say
Mike Forbester	Maura Shannon
Patricia Halliday	Henry Spence
Susan Harvey	Josephine Spence
Lucy Jackson	Jethro Standley
Karen Keay	Father Timothy Swinglehurst
Paul Keay	Rosalie Treble

Printed in Great Britain
by Amazon